NATIONAL AVENUE

Published by

SOUTH SHORE PRESS
6361 SOUTH 27TH STREET
SUITE 16
FRANKLIN, WI 53132
USA

Library of Congress Catalog Card Number
96-92516

ISBN No. 9654307-0-7

Cover Art by Stephanie Lansford

To My Children
Harley, Grace, Sonja,
Bruce and Claudia

❧

Thank you!

To all my friends at Writers' Ink who listened, questioned, criticized, offered suggestions and advice and otherwise encouraged and inspired;

To May Thibaudeau and Sharon Addy who had the courage to read through the entire raw manuscript, and to Linda Steele and Carla Bodette of the Nitpickers;

To Scott J. Piemeisel of Tri-City Bank, Oak Creek, Wisconsin, for his aid in removing some obstacles to the book's becoming a reality; and

To Harold E. Larson, benefactor (deceased.)

❧

NATIONAL AVENUE

by L. L. Larson

Chapter 1

"*Lindy?*"

I stomped my heel into my boot hearing my name above the babel in the crowded space around my locker.

"Here's that *Movie Star News* I said I'd pass along to you."

"Oh, thanks, Marjorie," I said, buttoning my coat. "Put it in the brieafcase with my homework, will you, please? Nice of you to remember."

"It's an old issue. Look, October, 1930. Four months old! Kind of battered. I got it from a girl in my French class." She pulled on her mittens. "I'll walk as far as your bus stop with you. Somehow it doesn't seem so cold if I have company. Hey! Is that a new coat?"

"Yeah." I answered penitently.

"Good looking coat! Whatsa matter? Don't you like it?"

"Yeah, I like it."

"You don't sound very enthusiastic. I'd be rapturous if I had a new coat."

"I guess I feel a little guilty about it. I feel out of place with a new coat when everybody around me is~" I didn't want to say *poor*. Marjorie's family, like thousands of others, was getting help from the county.

"Well, you know how hard things are for everybody now."

"Yeah, I know, but~Jimminy! You needed the coat."

"I sure did. My old one was so short! The sleeves were almost up to my elbows. I've had that coat since I was thirteen, I guess. That's about four years!"

"Don't feel guilty about a new coat," Marjorie scolded. "Gonna study tonight?" she asked as we shouldered the heavy door open into the cold.

"I don't know how much studying I'll do," I said. Our boots scuffed along the bare sidewalks where the snow had been shoveled. "My mother and I are going to have supper with Aunt Belle and Uncle Frank at their place tonight. They've just moved back to town."

"Are they the ones you told me about who went to Michigan or someplace out there looking for a job?"

"Yeah, they're the ones."

"Couldn't find any work there either, huh?"

"Nope."

"Gee! They sold all their stuff, too, didn't they?"

"Yup."

"Where are they living now? What are they doing?"

"They rented a couple furnished rooms on National Avenue and applied for county relief. That's what my mother told me. Aunt Belle is her sister, you know. That's all I know. I haven't seen 'em since they got back. I'm anxious to see 'em."

"You like 'em, don't you? You're pretty fond of 'em."

"Yeah. I sure do."

"Hey! Here comes your bus! That wasn't such a long wait."

"See ya tomorrow!"

"'Bye!" Marjorie waved. "Tell me about it tomorrow."

❁　　❁　　❁

My fingertips were numb with cold inside my gloves as I stood on the public sidewalk and looked at that blackened old mansion. I set my briefcase down and grudgingly removed one glove. With stiff fingers, I dug from my purse the note Mother had given me before I left home that morning.

1840 West National Avenue. This must be the place. No apartment number. Typical of Mother.

A weathered sign mounted on the lawn, identical to many throughout the city, announced that the property was for sale by the First National Trust Co.

In the dusk of this January day in 1931, the old house looked nothing like the mansion it had been. Once a bright Cream City brick, the house was now black with age and the residue of commerce which flowed past what remained of its broad lawn after the encroachment of the used car lot next door.

Picking up my brief case, I accosted the chevron brick walk with all the courage I could muster. It had been cleared of snow and was flanked by a leafless hedge. The deep porch, which stretched across the entire front, tilted forward. Even the cement-block pillars supporting its sagging roof showed signs of age where alternating extremes of winter and summer weather had caused chinks to appear in the cement which held them together. A wooden sign swung from metal eyes across the center:

LIGHT HOUSEKEEPING ROOMS

The double No. 18 streetcar growled past as I walked up the steps. A large card with a crayon message was tacked to the front door:

> Manager
> Apt. 1
> Around the back.

With my heavy briefcase, I trudged around the snow-covered foundation plantings to the rear of the building. As I approached the back door, I heard a loud male voice delivering a tirade of abuse followed by a shrill response. I felt goosebumps rise on my flesh. A family fight? *Oboy! Why this place?*

Timidly I mounted the stoop and knocked, shivering as much

from apprehension as from the cold. The seconds ticked by. The argument continued. While my heart thumped solidly in my chest, I deliberated whether to knock again or leave when I heard heavy footsteps inside.

The door opened. Before me stood a fat man chewing a mouthful of food. A few strands of black hair lay in disarray across his bald head. He wore bib overalls over his long-sleeved underwear. I could see the hair on his chest where two top buttons were missing. Having lived only with my mother for all of my nearly seventeen years, I had never before seen a man in such a state of undress.

At first he viewed me with suspicion. Then he looked me over greedily, a suggestive leer playing about his features. Beginning at my brimmed hat, his eyes rested on each brass button of my new, double-breasted, navy blue coat, past the fashionable hemline to the tips of my boots. "Whadaya want?" he asked while chewing.

"I'm looking for Mr. and Mrs. Franklin Roemer, Belle and Frank Roemer. They're my aunt and uncle. They have rooms at this address."

The man turned toward his companion.

"SHUT THE DOOR! For Christ's sake!" I heard a woman's voice. "You're lettin' in all the cold."

"Anybody here name o' Roemer?" the man asked while almost closing the door.

"Who wants t'know?"

"There's a girl here lookin' for 'em."

"O, yeah. That must be the one the new tenant's been tellin' me about. Tall girl? With kinda red hair and blue eyes?"

"I dunno about her eyes, but she's a looker! Yeah!"

"Well,—she's young," I heard the woman say bitterly. "She ain't had to put up with the likes o' you yet. That's Mrs. Roemer's niece. *Well!* don't make her stand out there in the cold, ya damned fool! Tell 'er to come in. The Roemer's are in **4.**"

The man waved me inside and closed the door behind me. I felt awkward and self-conscious. Aunt Belle must really have given her a mouthful about me.

Getting in out of the cold felt good. The smells of coffee and cigarettes permeated the place. We stood in a hall just inside the door. Straight ahead was a stairway. The large kitchen was on my right. Glancing in, I caught sight of the woman. She sat at the table in a faded bathrobe, which seemed odd considering the early evening hour. Her blond hair hung loose and tangled, the dark roots visible. She had pushed a soiled dinner plate aside and was applying very red lacquer to her fingernails.

"Go right up the stairs," she directed. "The Roemers live in the front apartment, number *4.* You shoulda went to the front door. It woulda been closer."

"I didn't know their number," I explained.

"I see. Well, you'll find 'em up there in *4.*"

At the top of the stairs, I found a door on my right marked *7.* Turning left, I passed the open door of a large bathroom. The strong scent of Lifebuoy was not enough to mask the odor of urine.

I wrinkled my nose. The floor creaked with every step. *Criminy! What a dump!* I thought. I found it hard to believe that Aunt Belle and Uncle Frank had been brought to this.

Continuing past *6* on my left, where a single bare bulb illuminated the windowless passage, I mounted three more steps at a little quirk in the hall, then past *5* on my right. Number *4* was a little beyond the top newel post of the front stairway. Looking over the banister, I could see the mosaic tiled floor of the entrance hall below.

Summoning my bravado, I rapped. Aunt Belle opened the door. She kissed my cheek and said, "Hello, Love. I see you found it all right. Are you frozen?"

"Well, I had to wait quite a while where I transferred to the streetcar but it was warm once I got inside."

Aunt Belle and my mother were sisters, both small, slender women with high cheek bones and straight noses. They strongly resembled each other except that Mother had dark, chestnut colored hair while Aunt Belle, the younger of the two, tended to be fair. I'd grown much taller than both of them. They said I must have got my height from my father's side of the family but, of course, I never knew.

"You're cold," Aunt Belle said taking my coat. "You have a new coat?"

"Yes," I said. "I kind of outgrew the old one."

"My! It's smart! So tailored. I like the brass buttons. Navy blue is such a practical color. Did the hat come with it? It's a perfect match."

"Yeah, it did. I like it. I think it will wear a long time," I said, trying to make it sound as though I wouldn't be getting another soon.

"You know," I said as I looked around, "this isn't a bad place." I had heard Mother lament her sister's hard luck. "I *love* the beautiful old fireplace. I can just imagine what a lovely old bedroom this was~"

"Yeah," Aunt Belle agreed. There was longing in her voice. "Marble."

"~and the beveled mirror above it. Beautiful!"

I tried to make it seem like something elegant. But with rag rugs scattered around the worn, linoleum floor and a brown tube-steel double bed occupying the middle of the room, the odds were against me.

I stroked a china bulldog on the mantle, a familiar nicknack from their former home, and was consoled. The aroma of sauerkraut and spareribs filled the apartment contributing to the homeyness Aunt Belle had somehow been able to bring into these dismal rooms. I followed her into the tiny kitchen which had once been a huge wardrobe and dressing-room adjunct to this once-master bedroom which now served as their living quarters. A built-in double chifforobe served admirably as kitchen storage space. Two long, narrow windows looked out onto the street.

The little table had been laid for four. Aunt Belle had covered the oilcloth with one of her white linen tablecloths, a relic of better times when she and Uncle Frank had had a cottage on the edge of town. After Uncle Frank's job in the foundry fizzled and they had exhausted their resources, they sold their household possessions and traveled to Flint and Detroit, Michigan, in search of work in the automotive industry. Their efforts proved futile and they were now back in Milwaukee, their money gone, worse off than before.

A pot of potatoes boiled gently on the four-burner gas plate. Aunt Belle had had lots of practice making an appetizing meal out of very little.

"Where's Uncle Frank?"

"He's next door~out on the lot~trying to sell some cars."

I looked out on the used car lot of the Schindler Ford agency next door. A string of bulbs hung across the front of the lot to illuminate the merchandise while a single bulb, one of those clear, blue, "daylight" kind, gave off an eerie light from the shack in the middle of the lot. The new car salesmen worked from the brick and glass showroom on the corner.

"How's he doing?" I asked. "Having any luck?"

"He talks about prospects." .

"When did he get that job?"

"It's not a job, really," Aunt Belle explained. "It's strictly commission. They allow him to hang around, and if he sells one, they'll give him a little something."

"Kind of a self-made job," I volunteered.

"You might say that."

"When's my mother coming?"

"She should be here any minute now."

"How long does the lot stay open?"

"Until nine."

"Will Uncle Frank have supper with us?"

"Yes, he'll come in to eat and then go right back out again."

"It's cold out there. Do they have a heater in that shack?"

"A little kerosene stove. It uses up all the oxygen. Then the condensation runs down the walls. They have to open it up then to get some fresh air inside.

"I think he's foolish to sit out there all those hours in the cold," Aunt Belle continued. "He'll get pneumonia and die here in this roominghouse."

There was a soft rap at the door and then it opened. My mother swept into the room wearing a fur coat. The cold, fresh air which swirled around her was scented with cologne. She was carrying a bag of groceries.

She's here! Her presence equated safety, comfort, love. She was my rock. She was perfect. She *had* to be perfect. I would not tolerate any imperfection in her.

"Mm-mm! So good to see you." She hugged Aunt Belle, then kissed my cheek.

"Thanks, Liz," Aunt Belle said as she took the bag from my mother. "You needn't have gone to the trouble. The County doesn't give us caviar or T-bones, but there's always enough. I baked bread today."

"Baked bread?" my mother asked incredulously as she removed her boots and set them out in the hall. "How could you do that without a stove?"

"O, a little magic," Aunt Belle replied playfully. "I have this little portable oven I use right on top of the gas plate. See?"

She showed us the little metal box with a rack inside and a door on the front. She also showed us the bread— two lofty loaves— bronzed to perfection. We were amazed.

Aunt Belle took the bag into the kitchen and removed some fresh fruit and a package of meat. Opening the window, she put the meat in a wooden box attached to the sill outside, then closed the window. "It will keep better frozen," she commented. "What's this?"

She extracted a flat paper bag from the bottom of the grocery bag. Inside a tissue was a new pair of silk stockings for Aunt Belle.

"O, Liz! You really shouldn't do things like this. It makes me feel so obligated."

"Nonsense!" Mother answered. "You've already done as much for me and more."

Aunt Belle hurriedly put the stockings in her dresser drawer. "I don't want Frank to see them," she said. "And don't say anything about the groceries, either," she cautioned. "You know, living from hand to mouth like this is very hard on him. He's always been so proud."

"O, bullshit!" Mother exclaimed, taking off her fur coat. "He's no better 'n the rest of us. We're all in the same boat."

"Leave him his pride," Aunt Belle admonished Mother defensively. "Don't take that away, too. Besides, we're *not* all in the same boat. *You* seem to be doing pretty well."

Mother snickered behind her hand. "I know," she said mischievously. "It's not me, really. It's Harve. He's doing all right. As long as he does okay, I will, too."

The two women exchanged knowing glances, then said no more. Aunt Belle went to the kitchen to check the potatoes as Uncle Frank whizzed through the door.

He was a slim fellow in his forties and only a little taller than I—five feet ten or thereabouts. He wore a small, dark mustache and worked in his only suit now that he had become a used car salesman. That was quite a change for him because he had always been a foundry hand before the mill went under. By temperament a happy, breezy guy, he was exuberant tonight.

"Hi, Liz! Hello, Lindy!" he greeted us, suppressing his enthusiasm long enough to place his hat on the mantelpiece with care. While still wearing his overcoat, he held my face between his cold hands and kissed me. Uncle Frank had doted on me as long as I could remember. Aunt Belle would never have any children of her own.

Always meticulous about his clothes, he put his coat on a hanger, then hung it on a pegged board which had been affixed to the wall beside the door. In the same way, he removed his suit coat, bantering conversation all the while.

"Bygod! I think I mighta sold a car today. Fella's gonna talk it over with his wife and maybe come back tonight."

"Really?" Aunt Belle called from the kitchen while getting the supper on the table.

Smiling, Uncle Frank wandered into the kitchen while carefully turning up his shirt cuffs. I followed and saw him lovingly pat her behind before putting an arm around her shoulders and kissing her as she stood at the gas plate.

"Yeah. Y'know that green Studebaker coupe that came in a couple o' days ago?"

"O," Aunt Belle said, expressing good-natured impatience, "you remember all those cars. You work with 'em every day. But, no, I don't remember. Is that the one he's interested in?"

"Yup, that's the one."

"Well," Mother interjected, having followed me into the kitchen, "I sure hope you sell it. It would be a feather in your cap with the agency even if it doesn't pay much."

Uncle Frank's smile vanished. "It would pay pretty good," he said reprovingly as we squeezed into our chairs around the table in the cramped space. "That's a '28. It's almost new—only three years old—and it's in very good condition." He went into his sales pitch telling us about the mileage, the condition of the tires, the battery, and on and on.

I could see Mother wished she had never made that remark.

"Schindler's asking three hundred 'n' fifty bucks for it. I'd get ten per cent. Let's see" he considered. "That'd be thirty-five bucks! That'd be better'n a week's wages at the foundry."

Aunt Belle looked proud. "We'd have to report it to the County then, wouldn't we?"

"I s'pose," Uncle Frank admitted. "But, Christ! Excuse me, Honey," he apologized to me, "I'd rather pay my own way than get it from the County anyway. It would be nice to pick out our own groceries for a week, wouldn't it?"

She handed him the potatoes. "Sure would."

"I'd like some of that homemade bread," Mother said.

"How's Harve doing? Where is he tonight?" Uncle Frank asked Mother.

"He's on his way to Atlantic City."

"Bringing back another load?"

"I guess so. He doesn't say too much but I know."

Uncle Frank shrugged. "Doesn't he worry that he might get arrested—or worse?"

"I suppose he does. But that's where the money is. In times like these, you can hardly blame a person."

"I believe prohibition is a good law," Aunt Belle put in. "God knows booze has caused a lot of misery. But they will never be able to enforce it."

"Haven't been able to up to now," Uncle Frank agreed.

Harve? Bootlegging? It was the first I'd heard of it. Mother had been dating Harve for about a year now. I had a vague idea that he was a salesman of sorts, but got the impression that what he sold was beyond the concerns and comprehension of a sixteen-year-old girl. I visualized some kind of hardware.

"Too bad he has to go way down there for it. I should think he'd rather do business closer to home. Like Chicago."

"Harve doesn't want to get mixed up with the Chicago boys. They play rough. Remember the Valentine's day massacre just last year? Or was it the year before?"

"The year before. 1929. It's January now. 'Member? 1931 already," Uncle Frank reminded us.

"That's right! Anyway, he's trying to keep his little business to himself. He's a small operator. Sells to a couple of speakeasies on the edge of town and down in the ward. He's making a good living for himself. At least he's not asking the County for anything."

My face burned. *Mother, how could you?* I saw the hurt in Uncle Frank's face. I felt Aunt Belle's pain as she empathized with him.

But it was typical of Mother. We all were aware of it--this blind insensitivity that trampled roughshod over tender feelings.

Oblivious to the wreckage in her wake, Mother continued. "From what I've been able to gather, this is off-shore stuff--from Jamaica. Good rum. They motor out past the three-mile limit to pick it up, then bring it back in small private launches and sell it to guys like Harve."

"What about the Coast Guard?" Uncle Frank asked. "Don't they go after 'em?"

"They don't have the equipment. Too slow. The private launches are much faster."

"What if he gets picked up along the way home?"

"A bottle usually takes care of it."

Bribery! I was appalled.

Uncle Frank said, "Hmm." Then, suddenly putting down his napkin, he pushed his chair away from the table making a scraping noise on the floor. "God! That was good, Belle," he announced. "I'm sorry I have to leave you ladies, but I have to get back to the lot. I just might have a customer tonight." He walked out of the apartment and down the hall toward the bathroom.

"The bread was delicious, Belle," Mother commented as we rose to clear the table. "I swear, you're a genius in the kitchen."

Uncle Frank now stood at the door, buttoning his coat. Appraising his image in the mirror above the marble fireplace, he adjusted the brim of his fedora over his right eye, giving him a dapper look. Aunt Belle smiled admiringly and kissed him. "Goodbye, Love," she said. "And good luck! I hope you sell that car."

"Wouldn't that be swell?" He winked and snicked his tongue.

❧❧

Chapter 2

Mother and Aunt Belle had become engaged in a lively discussion while clearing the table. I was angry, so I got out of the kitchen. With my shoes off, I propped myself up on the bed, punched the pillows a few whacks, and opened my *Modern American History*. I must have read about the assassination of Archduke Franz Ferdinand a dozen times without retaining anything. *My mother!* Associating with a *bootlegger!*

I gave up, threw the history book aside and picked up the *Movie Star News*. While continuing to fume, I absently flipped through it. A full-page sepia photo of Norma Shearer, 1930 Academy Award winner, caught my attention. I read the accompanying article and was amazed by the style of life described. Photos of her home in Beverly Hills pictured interiors of spacious rooms of varied ambience: a gracious reception area, a winding staircase, a dining room of impressive proportions, a card room, a breakfast nook. Small, intimate rooms with delicate brocade-upholstered chairs for tea in precious, eggshell-thin china cups, glass shelves on which were displayed small and exquisite artifacts.

An aerial view highlighted the graceful lines of the stone and brick residence. Set on a rolling velvet lawn, its swimming pool shimmered like a jewel in California's perpetual sunshine.

Photos of Ethel Merman and Ruth Etting and stories of their fabulous incomes made me indignant. That someone would be paid such stupendous amounts of money—hundreds of dollars—for doing something so *easy* was unbelievable to me. For *singing!* Why, *anybody* can sing! You just open your mouth and there it is!

I thought of Aunt Belle and Uncle Frank living in this squalid place while these people earned sinful amounts of money for *playing!* Why there so *much* and here so *little?*

And *my mother!* Dating a *bootlegger!* And *myself*—unprepared for history class tomorrow. Who cared about Archduke Franz Ferdinand anyway? He was dead. But I was *alive—here and now.* What about *me?*

What if *I* was discovered? What if it happened to *me?*

From some remote planet I heard Mother say, "C'mon, Lindy. We'd better be getting home."

I glanced out toward the lot one last time before putting on my coat. I saw a couple examining a car with interest. From inside the shack, Uncle Frank had seen them, too. He came forward to greet them.

"I think Uncle Frank's prospect is out there now," I told Aunt Belle.

She came to the window, too. Mother stood behind us. Aunt Belle turned out the light so we would not be seen watching. The minutes dragged.

"C'mon, now," Mother urged. "Let's go."

"*Okay!*" I said.

"Yeah, this could take a while," Aunt Belle agreed.

We left Aunt Belle in the dark looking out the window, her small face illuminated by the bright lights of the car lot below. Uncle Frank and the couple were still negotiating as we walked past toward the Car Stop on 20th Street.

Waiting in the cold for the noisy old streetcar did nothing to improve my disposition. We dropped our coins in the fare box and settled into the yellow rattan seat. I sulked. Mother seemed not to notice, which irked me even more.

We were waiting for a red light at Twenty-seventh Street when she said, "My, you're quiet tonight."

"Been thinking."

"You sound serious."

"I guess I am."

"What's bothering you?"

"O, a lot of things, I guess."

"THIRTY-THIRD STREET," the motorman called from his perch at the front of the car.

We had to walk a block from the carline. Mother and I had an effeciency apartment just north of National on Thirty-third. The snow squeaked under our boots. We pulled our collars up around our throats and pulled our shoulders forward.

"Is something wrong at school?" she asked, her breath exploding into clouds with every word.

"Nope."

"What is it?"

"I didn't know Harve was bootlegging."

"I don't understand," Mother said. "What does that have to do with you? It doesn't effect *you* in any way."

"Yes, it does."

"How?" she said, taking the key from her purse as we approached the apartment building.

"Well, *Mother!* It's against the law."

"It's a poor law."

We did not resume our conversation until after we were inside our own apartment lest we be overheard~possibly even reported.

"I'm surprised at you, Lindy. I can't understand why you should concern yourself with such matters. Everyone recognizes that it's a poor law."

"It's not a poor law!" I shot back. "Booze is no good for anyone! It just makes a lot of trouble! It should be outlawed—and it is! I don't think you should be associating with Harve! I thought he was a decent person!"

I began to cry while hanging up my new coat in the closet space behind the rollaway bed.

Mother looked as though I had hit her in the solar plexus. Her mouth hung open as she looked at me in bewilderment.

"Why, Lindy Honey, I can't believe this! Harve is a good person. He wouldn't hurt anyone. He's been awfully good to me—and to you, too. Surely you must know that."

"T-to *me*? I asked.

"Yes, to you. He's paying the rent for this apartment, you know. And where do you suppose your new coat came from? Or mine?"

The full impact of our situation struck me. As she struggled to pull the rollaway bed from the closet, I threw myself on the sofa and bawled. Pushing her aside as she attempted to comfort me, I wailed and sobbed until my throat ached.

Mother had opened the pullman kitchen and put on a pot of coffee. The aroma of percolating coffee had a placating effect on my tumultuous emotions.

Dependent as I was, I felt trapped, torn between love and hate for the only person in the world I felt close to. I needed her desperately—needed the comfort that only she could give me in this moment of disillusionment. Yet, I was repelled by her. She had suddenly become repugnant to me—my *mother*. My *beloved* mother. In that moment it seemed that she died. The person standing before me was a stranger!

She set a cup of hot coffee on the end table beside me. Then taking a chair from beside the gate-leg table where we ate our meals, she sat opposite me with her cup in hand.

We both sipped for a few minutes, neither of us knowing which string to pull to begin untangling the knot before us. The coffee felt good to my aching throat. I began to cry again.

"Lindy, I had no idea you had such strong convictions about the law—about prohibition. What did you think Harve was doing?"

I told her what my impressions had been.

She reached for my hand. I drew it back. I wouldn't let her

touch me. I wanted my *mother*. My *other* mother. The one I knew until this evening.

"There's more to it than that," I accused.

"Well,—" she said, "out with it! As long as we're clearing the air—"

"Why is Harve doing all this for us? For you? What's he getting in return?"

Mother's face turned crimson.

"Lindy, we've been frank with each other up to now, haven't we?"

I agreed.

"We've gone over all the physical aspects of growing up—of reaching maturity, haven't we?"

I nodded. I knew what was coming. I didn't want to hear it. For several years now I had felt the yearnings, the irrepressible longings of my own body. I knew their stubborn, unsilenceable clamor. What's more, I knew she, too, knew. She'd made no complaint about my monopolizing the bathroom. She had seen through the subterfuge of my sudden concern with hygiene and grooming which was, in fact, a consuming curiosity about my developing anatomy.

"I don't have to spell it out for you, do I?" she continued.

"Mother, why do you do it? He's not your husband."

"Why do I do it? Because I need. Because he needs. Because we need each other."

I blew my nose.

"Why doesn't he marry you?"

"I don't know. When he's ready, he will."

"He may never be ready."

"Then I'm better off not being married to him. I know putting pressure on him will only drive him away. I'm not willing to risk that. Life is too short. I have to take my happiness where I find it."

"What do you know about him?"

"Not much. He was married. Lived out East. Pennsylvania, I guess. What came between them I don't know. There was one child—stillborn. If that had anything to do with it—I don't pry."

"Do you love him?"

"I don't allow myself to love him completely. I know he might be gone tomorrow. I could love him if—" Her voice trailed.

"If he'd marry you?"

She nodded.

I reflected on my own feelings for Matt Dorsey, a senior, football hero, honor roll, likely valedictorian. I recalled my self-conscious withdrawal when I encountered him in the hall surrounded by an admiring throng, afraid he could sense my compelling attraction to him.

Once our eyes met. Afterward I looked longingly at the back of his head in study hall, noting the smooth skin beneath his ear and wanting to touch him.

Again she reached for my hand. This time I took it and pulled her toward me. As the fragrance of her cologne washed over me, I hugged her tight as I had done so often as a child. In this gesture of mutual acceptance, I heard her say, "You see, Honey, I'm just a plain, old human being."

I got undressed and ready for bed, satisfied that I had my mother back. Not as she was, not as I had always perceived her, not the same mother, but my mother nevertheless.

Chapter 3

Marjorie was waiting at my locker when I arrived at school the next day.

"G'morning," she greeted me.

"Hi!" I replied while trying to find room for my boots and new coat in the dinky wooden locker, one of many which had not yet been replaced by the tall steel ones.

I was still burdened by the revelations of the previous day. I longed to talk about it, but~ While best friends didn't keep anything from each other, I felt a need to protect Mother in her illicit love affair with a man who was breaking the law.

"You sound a little glum," Marjorie noted.

It was an invitation to tell all, but I resisted.

"Didn't mean to," I said. "Everything's fine."

Marjorie was unconvinced, I knew, but being the sensitive, thoughtful person she was, she did not pursue it.

Marjorie and I looked a lot alike. She, too, was tall and even slimmer than I. Willowy, I guess you'd call her. Her hair was a rich brown color. Cut to a length just below the ear, it fell in soft waves around her face. Her eyes were wide and blue. We were sometimes taken for sisters~a misperception we both enjoyed.

"Staying for the basketball game tonight?" she asked.

"The basketball game?" I had forgotten about it. "Who're they playing?"

"Tech."

"Boys' Tech?"

"Yeah. Why don't you come?"

"I didn't tell my mother I'd be late."

"Call her up."

"Maybe at lunch time," I answered.

The five-minute bell rang.

"Okay, see you then," she said, and walked toward her first hour class.

Basketball! I thought. *The world is falling apart and she's thinking about basketball!*

As I walked toward my first hour class, I suddenly felt older than Marjorie—more mature. I also felt alienated from her, the same as I had felt toward Mother the night before.

I had English first hour with Mr. Russell Richmond. He was the newest teacher at the school having begun only two years before. He was young and handsome, and I, along with every other girl in the school, ached with longing just looking at him. He was about six feet tall, and his broad shoulders and erect posture gave him the bearing of a military officer.

As I entered the room, he stood before the class in a grey business suit, feet apart, hands clasped behind his back, watching the door for stragglers. His smile revealed good, well-cared-for teeth. His wavey blond hair shone with pomade. The boys, envious of his self-assured good looks, said he had a receding hairline. The girls, however, spoke of his high forehead as an indication of intellect.

He provided the necessary elements for us, the young women in his class, to unlock our romantic imaginations. His biography in the school newspaper mentioned his recent engagement to a teacher at another school. This was no deterrent to the sighs that escaped his students as he read in a sonorous baritone John Lyly's *Appeles' Song* or Shakespeare's *Sonnet CXVI:*

. . .

> *Love's not Time's fool, though rosy lips and cheeks*
> *Within his bending sickle's compass come;*
> *Love alters not with his brief hours and weeks,*
> *But bears it out ev'n to the edge of doom—. . .*

I seated myself and tried to give my full attention to the subject at hand but I found my mind wandering to the events of yesterday—thinking aimlessly about Harve, about Mother, and wondering if Uncle Frank had sold that car. He was so hopeful.

"Let's turn to page 322 in your *Literature and Life*," I heard Mr. Richmond direct.

It was an excerpt from *Henry Esmond,* by William Makepeace Thackeray, in which a man returns to his mistress and their young adult son. Silently I read:

> *They never had been separated. His*
> *mistress had never been out of his mind*
> *all that time. No, not once. No, not in*
> *the prison; nor in the camp; nor on shore*
> *before the enemy; nor at sea under the*
> *stars of solemn midnight; nor as he*
> *watched the glorious rising of the dawn;*
> *not even at the table, where he sat*
> *carousing with friends, or at the theater*
> *yonder, where he tried to fancy that*
> *other eyes were brighter than hers.*

I thought of my mother. Was I, too, the child of such a love affair? I stirred in my seat. The seat creaked. I glanced toward Mr. Richmond. Our eyes met. My face was hot. I dropped my gaze to the page. The clangorous warning bell broke the spell.

Mr. Richmond wrote our next day's assignment on the board and announced, "Class dismissed."

Two more classes and a study hall before fifth hour lunch.

By the time I met Marjorie at the cafeteria, I was starved.

"Hope they've got something good to eat today," I said as we stood in line. "I'm so hungry."

"Me, too," Marjorie admitted.

Boisterous male voices could be heard coming into the room. A political discussion had carried over from Miss Bradshaw's civics class again. Miss Bradshaw had a knack of stirring up sharply conflicting views. There was always a waiting list to get into her classes. Her students thrived on the exhilaration resulting from the rough-and-tumble of clashing ideas.

Taking his tray and walking backwards into the cafeteria line, the better to face his adversary as he pursued his point, was Matt Dorsey. He was still debating and gesticulating when he backed into me. As he spun to face me, he grabbed my shoulders to steady himself.

"Omigod! I'm sorry."

He recognized me. His face colored.

"It's okay," I said.

"Did I hurt you? I didn't hurt you, did I?"

"No, I'm all right."

Marjorie was giggling. I didn't look at her but I could tell.

"Geez!" Matt continued, "I didn't mean it."

"I know. It's okay. I'm all right."

"You're sure?"

"Positive."

I had been filling my tray during this exchange and, with Marjorie, now looked for a table. The boys followed us and seated themselves at a table nearby.

"Did you call your mother yet?" Marjorie asked.

"Call my mother? About what?"

"The basketball game."

"O, yeah. I almost forgot." I looked through my coins. "Shucks!" I said. "No nickel. Do you have a nickel?"

Marjorie went through the same ritual.

"No nickel," she announced.

A shadow fell across the table as a figure interrupted the light from the windows. We looked up into the face of Matt.

"Somebody need a nickel?" he asked, extending his hand in which he displayed a brand new, shiny 1930 nickel.

"I do," I said. "I have to make a phone call."

"Here you are, ma'am. With my compliments."

"Are you sure?"

"Sure I'm sure. I won't need it. Really. You can have it."

"Well, okay. I'll pay you back as soon as I get change."

"There's no need for that," Matt said as he pulled a chair away from the table and, folding his tall frame like a retractable jack, sat down. I detected humor and shyness in his hazel eyes as they engaged mine. I couldn't believe this was happening. For such a long time I had carried this secret crush. To think he might even notice me sent me to the stars.

"Here, give me the nickel," Marjorie suggested, sensing the significance of the moment, "I'll call your mother and tell her about the basketball game."

"Thanks," I said, still studying Matt's features, his brown, kind-of-curly hair. He wore a V-neck jacquard sweater over his light blue shirt.

Marjorie, took her purse and tray and left us gazing at each other.

"You going to the basketball game?" Matt asked.

"Yeah."

"Tonight—after school?"

"Yes. Marjorie and I thought we'd take it in."

"Gee, that's great. I'll see you there. Is that okay?"

"Sure, it's okay."

"Hey," he stole a glance around the cafeteria, "is it okay if I sit with you?"

"I guess so," I said. "You understand, of course, that Marjorie will be with me. We made plans to go together."

"Yeah, I know. Can I walk home with you?"

"I have a school pass. I take a bus."

"O, yeah?" he said with interest. "Where do you live?"

"Over on Thirty-third and Pierce."

"Thirty-third and Pierce? There's nothing over there but apartments."

"Yeah, I know," I said. "I live in one of 'em with my mother."

"You *do?* You *live* in one of 'em?"

The warning bell rang.

"Yeah," I said. "I live in one of 'em."

"Ha!"

He thought I was joking. I picked up my purse, my books and my tray. Matt unfolded and pushed the chair back to the table. He was easily six feet tall. I headed for *Business Training*.

"See you at the game," Matt said as we parted.

"See you there," I agreed.

❧

Chapter 4

Somehow I floated through the rest of the afternoon without bumping into anything. Marjorie was waiting at my locker when the last class ended at 3:10. She was full of questions. "What happened?"

"He's going to be sitting with us at the game," I said.

"Hey, what about me?"

"It's okay. He knows we planned to come together."

"You're sure it's okay?"

"Of course. What did my mother say?"

"She said it was all right for you to stay. She wanted to know why you didn't make the call yourself. I told her you were making out with a football hero."

"Marjorie, you didn't."

Marjorie laughed. "No, I really didn't. I just told her you were tied up in a conversation you couldn't break away from very–" She searched a moment, "–graciously."

"Thanks," I said. "You're a good friend."

Later, as we walked toward the gym, I told her Matt had asked to walk home with me. I really didn't expect him to ride the streetcar, though.

"Hey," Marjorie observed, "this guy doesn't waste any time, does he?"

We found our seats in the bleachers. The teams had already tipped off and the game was in progress. Our team had scored the first basket and kids were yelling and clapping, the noise reverberating in the hollow gym. Marjorie and I were caught up in the excitement of the game. The lead had changed hands so many times and so quickly that before we knew it, the first period was over. Matt hadn't come yet.

As second period got under way, I found I was less able to concentrate on the game. I began scanning the faces of spectators, hoping to find him and afraid I might. I sensed that Marjorie was also looking around. It would be humiliating to be dumped.

"Maybe he got tied up somewhere," she said.

"Yeah, maybe," I said, sure that I'd been ditched.

The fourth period had just begun. I wilfully gave my attention to the game, concentrating on every play. Tech had the ball. The scoreboard was in our favor by two points. Spectators were on their feet screaming while watching a magnificently controlled dribble march down the court. I became aware of someone squeezing past the spectators in our row. It was Matt.

"Bet you thought I'd dumped you," he said as we sat down. Everybody on the bleacher wiggled a little closer to make room.

"Well, I did wonder what was keeping you."

"I still have a paper route," he explained. "My dad doesn't want me to take on any more while I'm in school."

"He's smart."

"So—that's where I was."

"That's okay."

The crowd stood and cheered. Without knowing why, we joined them. I'm not sure who won that game. Usually Tech beat us.

"See you tomorrow," Marjorie called over her shoulder after we had squeezed through the crowded doorway. I waved.

Out in the hall, Matt was again the center of attention.

"Hi, Matt!" and "How's it goin', Matt?" were heard from every direction. He made smiling responses, tousling their colorful knitted caps and playfully punching their shoulders. Then taking my hand, he urged me toward the side door.

"Where're you going?" I asked.

"Going to take you home."

"Take me home?"

Out in the winter night, Matt took my hand and drew me toward a green Chevy coupe parked at the curb. When he opened the door for me, I felt my scalp prickle.

"O, Matt!" I exclaimed, "I don't know. I'd better take the bus as usual. I don't think my mother would approve."

"But, Lindy!~" he argued. It was strangely thrilling to hear him say my name. "The real reason I was late tonight is so I could borrow my brother's car just to take you home—so you wouldn't have to freeze waiting for the bus and the streetcar."

"Why, Matt," I said, thoroughly humbled. "I had no idea—Of course, I'll go with you."

I got into the strange vehicle and heard the door slam. Matt came around and took his place behind the wheel. He handled the car with the aplomb of an experienced driver.

"How long have you been driving?" I asked.

"O, about two years. Since I was sixteen."

"You seem to drive very well."

"There's not much to it. I bet you could learn."

"Me?"

"Yeah. You could. Some women drive."

"I've seen a few, but not many," I said.

I couldn't believe I was sitting there beside him. The last time I'd been in a car I had been with Mother and Harve.

As we drew up to a stop light, I said, "Where are we? This isn't the way to my house."

"Just going for a little ride."

I remembered Marjorie's comment, *This guy doesn't waste any time, does he?*

"It's already past supper time," I said. "I can't be too late. My mother will worry."

"It's such a pretty night," Matt observed. "I thought we might walk through the park."

"Which park?"

"That one named for the Revolutionary War hero. It's a Polish name. I can't pronounce it, but you know."

"Yeah, I know. I can't pronounce it either. Well," I considered, "I can't be out too long. Besides, I'm getting hungry."

"I know. Me, too."

He parked at the curb, then opened the door for me.

"It really is a lovely evening," I remarked, "I think it's warmer than it was this morning."

"January thaw. A taste of spring," he said, taking my arm.

We walked silently for a time. The snow lay on the bare, black trees. Our boots crunched on the snowy walkway, our breath visible. The white lights emanated a ghostly glow over the silent scene. Placing an arm around my shoulders, Matt took my hand and pulled it around his waist. I matched his gait. I was glad for my long legs, even though Mother and Aunt Belle despaired, believing that tall women were less feminine.

"What are you thinking?" Matt asked after a long silence.

Could I tell him I was thinking of Mother and Aunt Belle? What were they doing here, anyway?

"I was thinking about how well I match your gait. We walk well together, don't you think?"

"I hadn't thought about it, but—yes, we do."

We came to the frozen lagoon. A few skaters were on the ice. We watched as some practiced their figure eights while others skimmed effortlessly in long, pleasurable strides.

"Do you skate?" he asked as we turned to walk back to the car.

"No, I've never tried it," I grudgingly admitted.

"Would you like to?"

"I don't have any skates."

"Could you borrow a pair?"

"The only person I know well enough to ask is Marjorie, and she wears a smaller size."

"I have two sisters," he said. "Maybe there's a pair around home that would fit you. What size do you wear?"

O, *no!* I thought, remembering Mother again with her size four-and-a-half.

"Eight," I admitted shyly.

"I'll find out," he said. "It sounds a little small. I think she wears a nine. You have to have room for warm socks. Do you have any wool socks?"

"Nope, never needed any."

We were back at the car.

"I'm starving," I complained.

"There's a White Tower just a couple blocks from here on Lincoln. Would you like a hamburger?"

"No, I'd better not. I know my mother is wondering what happened to me."

"I s'pose mine is, too."

I held my breath when the cold car protested a few times, wondering what Mother must be thinking. When, at last, it started, belching clouds of exhaust into the night air, I relaxed in my seat. We sat still for a few moments, "to let the engine warm up," Matt said.

It was the dinner hour in this blue-collar, working-class neighborhood. Lights glowed warmly in the windows of the frame flats which bordered the park. The quiet, residential street was deserted.

Before releasing the brake, Matt turned toward me and embraced me. His lips were warm and soft. I felt myself open to him like a flower to the rain. Again and again, I tasted his sweetness. Then, breathing audibly, he turned his attention to traffic and drove me home. The moment engraved itself on my memory, never to be forgotten.

As we approached our apartment building, I caught a glimpse of

Mother behind the glass door. She was waiting in the vestibule, wearing her brown sweater. She had turned up the thick shawl collar and, with her arms across her chest, thrust her hands inside the sleeves.

She watched us get out of the car. When she was sure it was I, she turned and went back into the apartment. Matt, of course, didn't know she was my mother, if he saw her at all.

He left the engine running and came to the door with me. "Gee," he worried, "I hope I didn't get you into any trouble with your ma."

"I do, too. We get along pretty well. I'm sure she'll understand," I said, remembering our discussion just last night.

"I sure hope so," he said. "If I can get hold of some skates for you, would you like to try ice-skating—say, Sunday afternoon?"

"I'd like that very much."

"I'll be in touch with you at school," he said as he turned toward the little car. "Gee!" he said, looking back at the building. "I never knew anybody who lived in an apartment building before."

෴

Chapter 5

I didn't know how Mother would react to this foray off the beaten path. Nothing like this had ever happened before. The door to our apartment was slightly ajar. I pushed it open. Mother was in the kitchen, attending to kettles on the range.

"Hi!" I called, trying to conceal the elation I was feeling. "I'm home." I hung up my coat.

"Hello."

Her voice was controlled. I wasn't sure if she was hurt or angry. I helped get dinner on the table.

"Was it a good game?"

"Yes, very exciting."

She handed me a steaming bowl of vegetable-beef stew.

"Mm-mm! That smells good. I'm so hungry."

"I should think you would be. It's almost two hours past our usual dinner time." She took the bowl from me. "Who won?"

"I guess Tech."

"Don't you know?"

"Well, the lead changed hands so often~"

"Were you there?"

"Was I *there*? Of course I was there."

She was questioning my veracity. She had never done that before. What was happening to us?

"I saw you come home in a car."

"I know. I saw you."

"Who's the young man?"

"A kid from school."

"He drives to school? He must be a rich kid. I didn't know there were any rich people on the south side."

"Mother! If you'll just stop cross-examining me—It's not his car. It's his older brother's car. It's nothing to worry about."

I tried to reassure her but I wasn't too sure myself. My mind darted back to the ecstatic moment when—I was still aglow.

"Have you known him a long time?"

"Well," I hesitated, "yes and no."

"What kind of an answer is that?"

"We've been seeing each other in the halls for a couple of years, but we were never introduced or anything. He isn't in any of my classes—so we never spoke to each other—until today, that is."

"O? What happened today?"

"He backed into me while we were standing in the cafeteria line. He didn't really hurt me, but he apologized. Over and over again. Later, he heard Marjorie and me looking for a nickel so I could call home and tell you I'd be a little late tonight."

I began to giggle remembering. She didn't laugh with me as she usually did. She just looked very serious and a little angry.

"So—what happened?"

"Well,—" I chuckled again. She was growing impatient with me. "Neither of us had a nickel, so he came over to our table and gave me a nickel." The suppressed laughter bubbled forth. It seemed so funny—such a trifling thing—a *nickel!* I laughed and laughed—until the tears flowed. My spirits were so high, I felt I was floating just beneath the ceiling—right over her head.

I covered my face with my napkin and, wiping my eyes, brought myself under control.

Mother still looked very stern. I didn't understand it.

"Well!" she said, "I hope you understand that I was worried sick about you. I hope you won't do that again."

"Do what?"

"Be so late for supper without letting me know."

"Why, Mother! I let you know. I called you at lunch time and told you I'd be late. And I was late. Isn't that letting you know?"

"Now, see here, young lady! You know very well what we're talking about."

"Oh? What are we talking about?"

"I'm talking about riding in cars with young men—about all the petting and necking that goes on. It just gets girls in trouble."

My jaw dropped as I stared at her in disbelief.

"Mother! How dare you say such a thing to me! Your own daughter!"

"My own daughter is just as vulnerable as anybody else's daughter. I'm just trying to protect you."

Protect me? From *Matt?* But I *wanted* Matt!

The hot tears burned my eyes and then spilled over. In an instant, she had turned my beautiful memory into something cheap and shoddy. As easily as I had laughed a few moments before, I now cried. To be so maligned by one I loved and trusted was hurtful beyond belief.

As I sobbed into my napkin, I visualized myself in a boxing ring and took a few jabs at Mother. Just *who* did she think she *was?* Protecting *me?* From *what?*

The whirlwind created by these mental calisthenics swept out the corners of my brain and swirled before me what I had not seen before. *She was trying to protect me from her own experience!*

I was torn with conflict. While still smarting under the sting of her remarks, I knew they sprang from her deep love for me. I rose from the chair and began to clear the table, sniffling and blowing from time to time.

"I'm trying to understand," I said.

"So am I," she answered.

We washed dishes in silence. Then I took up my usual position at the gateleg table, with my books and a lamp, to do my assignments. Mother read the evening newspaper. After finishing the written work, I took my history book to the sofa and tried to study.

Concentration was impossible. The emotional roller coaster of the last two days had exhausted me. I fell asleep. When I awoke, Mother had taken the rollaway from the closet and was preparing to retire. I did the same.

＊　　＊　　＊

We'd fallen into a morning pattern. Being a little taller than Mother, I could more easily put the rollaway back into the closet. She made breakfast—usually in her bathrobe. Neither of us was talkative until we'd had our morning coffee. Even as a small child, I had had coffee for breakfast.

"I talked to Aunt Belle yesterday," Mother said, breaking the silence.

"O? Did Uncle Frank sell that car? I thought about him several times yesterday."

"Yes, he sold it. They're feeling good about that."

"That's good. Is everything else okay?"

"Well, the couple who's been managing the rooming house has been fired."

"Fired?"

"Aunt Belle said the fighting went on until all hours of the night. Disturbed everybody in the building. The police were there a couple times. They didn't take very good care of the place anyway.

"Mr. Justus, the trustee for the Trust company, came to inspect the premises. He talked to the tenants. Then he asked Aunt Belle and Uncle Frank to manage the building. Of course, they were overjoyed to get such a break.

"Anyway, it will mean Aunt Belle and Uncle Frank will be moving into the apartment downstairs. They'll have a lot more room. There's a big kitchen, a combination living and dining room with a kind of a sun parlor at one end, and a big bedroom with windows on three sides on the other side."

"Windows on three sides?"

"Yes. Belle was told the bedroom was originally a conservatory. The apartment stretches across the whole width of the house."

"My!" I exclaimed. "What will they furnish it with?" I remembered they had sold all their household goods.

"The furniture stays. It's part of the package."

"How lucky for Aunt Belle," I said, knowing how much she loved homemaking and how well she did it.

"Fortunate for Mr. Justus, too," Mother observed. "There's a lot of work to be done. Besides having a larger place of their own, they'll have the halls and the bathroom to keep clean, and Uncle Frank will take care of the furnace. That means shoveling coal and hauling ashes and generally being tied down. Of course, they don't go anywhere anyway. I guess the furnace is an old monster. It should be replaced, but they're just trying to keep it going long enough to attract a buyer."

"I suppose they'll have to shovel snow and cut grass, too."

"That's all part of it, I guess."

"They would have to do the same if they still had their own place," I commented as I put on my coat.

"True," Mother admitted, "but it would be their own."

We kissed goodbye and I headed for the streetcar line.

❋   ❋   ❋

Matt was waiting at my locker when I arrived, which tickled me. It occurred to me that I hadn't mentioned the Sunday afternoon skating date to Mother.

"I think I've got a pair of skates for you," he said excitedly. "My sister outgrew 'em. My folks got her a new pair last Christmas. She says you can have 'em if you want 'em."

"Your sister is very generous. She doesn't even know me. Suppose I just borrow 'em and see how they fit."

"I got some socks for you, too. But they're just on loan. She wants 'em back."

"It looks as though you thought of everything."

The warning bell clanged.

"See you Sunday, one o'clock," he called over his shoulder as he left for his first class.

I caught a glimpse of Marjorie walking toward me.

"Okay," I called after Matt.

"Looks as though you two are getting along pretty well," Marjorie commented as Matt strode down the hall.

"Some day when there's more time, I'll tell you all about it," I promised as I hurried away.

✱   ✱   ✱

Tonight I must tell Mother about the Sunday afternoon skating date, I told myself as I stared through the streetcar window on the way home from school. I reviewed events of the previous evening. That Mother would put such lurid implications on Matt's driving me home disturbed me, particularly since she had excused her own intimacy with Harve on the grounds of "being human."

I let myself into the apartment with my usual greeting and hung up my coat.

"Hello, Honey," she answered dolefully from the kitchen. Her reddened eyes told me she'd been crying.

"What's the matter?"

"It's Harve."

"What about Harve?"

"He's in jail."

"In *jail?*"

"In jail," she answered stoically.

"Where?"

"In Cleveland. He got permission to call me long distance."

"Long distance?" It would have to be a real emergency to warrant a long distance call. "What did he say?"

"Said he had a little traffic accident and they caught him with the stuff. He doesn't have a whole lot of money with him. Had to pay for the load. Now the load's been confiscated by the Feds. I don't know what to do for him. I haven't anything. He said I shouldn't worry. Maybe one of his customers will help him out. I'll just have to wait and see."

"What about the rent?" I asked.

"What rent? O, you mean *our* rent?"

"Yes, *our* rent."

"I hadn't thought about it." She looked dismayed.

"Mygod, Ma! We have to think about ourselves!"

She thought a moment, then went to the dresser drawer and withdrew an envelope. There was money in it. I saw her riffle through some bills. Her lips moved as she counted.

"There's enough here to pay a month's rent and keep us in groceries until the end of the month if we're careful," she said. "We'd better give notice when we pay the rent."

"Give notice? Where are we going?"

"I don't know. Perhaps I should apply for Outdoor Relief. They may pay our rent if we find a cheaper place to live."

For a long moment, we looked at each other in silence.

"Well," she said at last. "Let's have supper."

❧❧

Chapter 6

I hated Saturdays. It meant getting up at almost the same time as during the week. There was always a full schedule laid out for me. I did the breakfast dishes while Mother gathered up the laundry. She packed everything into a laundry bag, along with a box of soap chips, and made her way to the basement. I was expected to vacuum and dust and clean the bathroom. I never understood why this had to be done on Saturdays when Mother was at home all week with very little else to do, but she had a theory that children should not be allowed to grow up without responsibility.

Washing, rinsing, wringing and hanging the laundry kept her downstairs until about noon when I, too, was finished with my chores.

Today, she came back just as I was setting lunch on the table.

"I thought we might go over to Aunt Belle's this weekend. She could probably use some help moving," she said.

"I plan to get my schoolwork finished this afternoon."

"You usually do that on Sundays."

"Not tomorrow. I promised to go ice skating."

"Ice skating? But you don't skate."

"Well, I'm going to try."

"You don't have any skates."

"I've arranged to borrow some."

She regarded me questioningly. "Oh? From whom?"

"From a friend of a friend, you might say."

"You're becoming so distant from me."

"Mother, I do have a life of my own. I know lots of people you don't know. I see 'em every day."

"Where do you plan to go skating?"

"Over at that park on Lincoln."

"Kosciusko?"

"I guess," I said. "I've never been able to pronounce it."

"It's quite a walk in the cold. You'll be frozen before you get there."

"I won't be walking," I said. "Matt is calling for me with his brother's car."

"Matt?"

"Yes. Matt. He's my friend—the one who brought me home after the basketball game."

"What about Aunt Belle?"

"What *about* Aunt Belle?"

"I just thought you might want to help her move."

"O, Mother! All they have to move is their clothes and some dishes. They're staying right in the same house. They don't need a truck or anything. I think they can handle it without me."

"I'd feel guilty about not helping her."

"Well, go ahead," I said impatiently. "There's no reason for *me* to be there. I have a key. I can let myself in when I get home."

"I don't like your tone, young lady," Mother said pompously.

I drew in my breath. "I'm sorry." I couldn't afford to upset her now. I wanted to keep that date more than anything in the world.

Sensing that she again had control of me, she said "That's better."

At that moment, I hated her. It would be four years until I was twenty-one! I didn't know if I could be subservient that long.

My face must have revealed my feelings for she turned sweet and repentant. "All right," she said. "I guess I'll have to recognize that you're not a little girl any more."

I noted with satisfaction that she now had to look up to me and I was thankful for my tall father, whoever he was. I promised myself then that if I ever found him, I would thank him for choosing ancestors with long legs.

"Thank you," I said with as much civility as I could muster, appreciating how much it had cost her to make that concession.

❀　　❀　　❀

We had an early dinner on Sunday. A little before one o'clock, I put on my coat, hat and boots and went out to the vestibule to wait for Matt. Mother left a few minutes later. I watched her walk toward the streetcar line on National Avenue. She was headed for Aunt Belle's. She hadn't heard anything more from Harve and she was brooding.

I recognized the little green Chevy at the curb and dashed out to meet it. Reaching across the seat, Matt opened the door for me and announced, "I've got the skates."

"O, thanks," I said with one foot on the running board as I clambered onto the seat beside him.

"The socks are in my pocket," he added as I pulled the door shut. "They're red. Hope you don't mind."

"Red ones will keep my feet warmer," I quipped happily.

It was a clear, beautiful day and I was at the park with Matt. Nothing else mattered. When the socks and the skates were comfortable, Matt helped me to my feet. Hanging onto his arm, I managed to walk the rough boards from the pavilion to the lagoon. When the blades made contact with the ice, they took off on their own leaving me sitting on the ice. Matt and a stranger helped me to my feet again. This time I had a better understanding of the medium I was to master.

Uncertain and shaky at first, I clung to Matt. He put his arm around my waist and taking my hand in his, he coached me into an easy glide.

"Relax," he urged. "You're too tense. I can feel that you're too tense." He hugged me toward him, his hand beneath my breast.

"Okay, I'll try."

"Tha-at's it. E-e-eazy does it!" His voice was soothing, resonant, reassuring.

I felt myself loosen and lean into the stroke. It was a delightful sensation. I laughed.

Smooth and rhythmic, we swept around the lagoon. It was a much larger lagoon than I had realized. After one turn around, I was more than ready to sit down on one of the benches at the edge of the ice.

"Getting cold?" he asked. His arm lay along the back of the bench, behind my shoulders. He squeezed me toward him as he spoke.

"A little."

"We can't sit still too long," Matt cautioned. "When it's cold, you have to keep moving. Have you had enough or do you want to try again."

"Since I'm here, I think I'll try again," I said with confidence and pride.

"Okay, let's go."

Later, Matt complimented me as we got into the car.

"Hey," he said, "for the first time out~" he snapped his fingers, "nothin' to worry about."

I was pleased with myself. I had given a respectable performance.

The car, warmed by the sun, started promptly. Matt allowed it to idle. When he turned toward me and gathered me into his arms, I yielded happily. We were in love. His coarse wool jacket, scratchy against my cheek, emitted a manly scent. While the winter sun hung on the western horizon, we held each other oblivious to the world around us. The western sky was pink and orange as we drove home.

"You know," Matt said on the way back, "I've never been in an apartment. What are they like?"

"Well, it's just one big room, really, with a sink and a gas plate and a little ice box behind two doors. We have a small bathroom."

"Where do you sleep?"

"There's a bed."

"It's a bedroom, then."

"No, it's a living room. And a dining room, too, I guess."

"And a dining room?"

"Yeah. We have a gateleg table that folds up almost flat against the wall when we're not using it."

"I'll be darned! What do you do with the bed?"

"It folds up and fits into the closet."

"Into the *closet?* I can't see it." He looked confused. "I just can't visualize it."

"Well," I said, "I have a key. Why don't you come in. I'll make some hot cocoa—if there's any milk."

"That sounds good."

He curbed the car and came into the building with me. As I stood before the door and, with cold fingers, fumbled for a key, Mrs. Leske across the hall opened her door. She looked at us, and then closed the door. Matt and I looked at each other with raised eyebrows and shrugged. After we were inside, Matt said "Is she nosey or something?"

"She's always been real nice to us as long as we've lived here." Then remembering how my own mother had put lewd implications on a simple automobile ride, I said, "Some folks always think the worst."

Matt's face reddened and he became uncomfortable. For a moment, we were both embarrassed. I took his coat and hung it in the closet, then my own. While he used the bathroom, I made two cups of hot cocoa. Standing beside me in the kitchen, he looked around with interest.

"Pretty ingenious!" he admitted. "You know, there really is a lot of space wasted in our house. When I compare this with my mother's kitchen—everything's so far apart. Nothing's handy."

We sipped the sweet, hot cocoa.

"This works pretty well for us," I said, although I hadn't given it any thought before.

"And the bed is in the closet, you say?"

"Yes. It's right here."

Setting my cup on an end table, I walked over and opened the double doors, exposing the underside of the bedspring.

"See?"

"I'll be darned!" Matt exclaimed. "I never saw anything like that. My ma should see this!"

I heard the key turn in the lock. Mother stepped into the room. Encountering Matt's tall, male presence, she was at once indignant and intimidated. Her face went pale. She looked from one to the other of us.

"Hi, Ma!" I said. "This is Matt. I was just showing him around the place."

"Never been in a place like this before," Matt said, extending his hand. "My ma would sure be surprised."

This reference to his mother changed her attitude and she shook his hand. "Yes," she said. "It's quite different from a regular house."

I had closed the closet doors on the bed.

"There's still a little cocoa in the pot. Would you like another cup?" I said to Matt.

"No, I promised my brother I'd get the car back to him by six. He has a date tonight."

"How many are in your family, Matt?" Mother asked.

"Four," Matt answered. "I have one brother and two sisters. By the way," he said turning to me, "if those skates fit you, you can have 'em."

"Why, Matt—" I said.

"O, no!" Mother put in. "We couldn't take 'em without paying for 'em."

"But she doesn't want anything for 'em. She got 'em from our cousin and they're too small now. You don't have to pay for 'em."

"Mother,~"

"Please don't interrupt, Lindy. In times like these, I suspect a family of six can use every penny."

Mother! I thought, *in times like these, we can't afford a pair of skates.*

As mother hung up her coat, Matt winked at me.

"All right," he said. "I'll take the skates back home with me."

I'd given Matt his coat and cap.

"Back home?" Mother said.

"Yes," he said. "I'll take 'em back." Then to me he said, "See you later, Lindy."

I followed him into the hall and walked to the chilly vestibule with him. We kissed as we said goodbye. Again I felt the same thrill as before.

"I'll take care of the skates," he said.

When I came back into the apartment, Mother was preparing supper. A thick Sunday edition of *The Milwaukee Journal* lay on the sofa. I browsed through it looking for the comics. That's when I found it! The ad! It jumped right at me. The Grayce, a neighborhood theater just two blocks away on National Avenue, was promoting a talent night. They were offering five dollars as a first prize and three dollars to the second place winner. The next three winners would be given theater tickets.

I had been given some solo parts in the school *a cappella* chorus, once in a general assembly on Armistice Day, but singing in a public theater~ *Should I try it?* Suppose there was a big Hollywood producer there? What if I was discovered? My heart raced. I was bursting with excitement!

I squelched the impulse.to tell Mother about it. I could tell by the sound of the dishes rattling in the kitchen that she was not in a receptive frame of mind. Finding Matt and me alone together in the apartment had unsettled her.

જી⅃ singles

Chapter 7

The strident ringing of the alarm clock invaded my dream disguised as the warning bell in Mr. Richmond's class. Still in the grip of sleep, I stumbled toward the bathroom surprised to smell coffee brewing. For Mother to be up, fully dressed, hair groomed and make-up in place at his early hour was highly unusual.

"Going someplace today?" I asked as I sat down to breakfast.

"Yes."

"Is it a secret?"

"No. I'll tell you. Remember the conversation we had the other day? About my association with Harve?"

"Yes."

"Well, I began to think about what a fragile thing it is. With Harve in jail, maybe I shouldn't be so dependent—

Maybe?

—so yesterday I bought a newspaper and looked at the classifieds. There's a job advertised that I think I can handle. I'm going to go today and apply."

"That's good news," I said, pleased that she took my views seriously. "What kind of a job is it?"

"A school for girls at the edge of town is advertising for a 'house mother' to live in the dormitory. They're offering sixty dollars a month and room and board."

"Room and board? You'd live right there? What happens to me?"

"Well, I haven't got the job yet," she reminded me, "but if I should get it, maybe we could work out some arrangement with Aunt Belle, now that she's going to have more room. We could give up this apartment—that's thirty dollars a month—and if I get room and board as part of my salary, everything I earn would be practically clear. I wouldn't even have any transportation expense."

"Boy! You've got it all figured out, haven't you?" I snapped angrily. "Don't I have anything to say about it?"

"You run along now, Dear. You'll be late." She urged me out the door. "We'll take one thing at a time."

I grabbed my briefcase and started toward the streetcar stop. I pulled my scarf up to my eyes as the bitter wind slashed at my face. The *Land o' Lakes* thermometer outside Blankstein's grocery store at the car stop indicated five below zero. I stamped my feet and wiggled my fingers to keep from freezing. The January thaw Matt had spoken of last week was short-lived.

I had no more got comfortable on the old double 18 when I had to get off and transfer to the bus which took me within a block of the high school, but it was long enough for me to reflect angrily on Mother's audacity in making decisions that affected me without any discussion at all. I was fond of Aunt Belle and Uncle Frank, but to live with them— I didn't know. I wondered how determined she was to investigate this job. Would she brave the cold today?

Marjorie was waiting for me at my locker when I came in. We both wore bright wool plaid skirts and sweaters. Marjorie had a white lace collar today. Mine was eyelet.

I envied Marjorie. It seemed that her life was so serene, so predictable. True, her father was unemployed, as so many were, but at least she knew who and where he was. They were getting some help from the county and, with odd jobs occasionally, they were getting by. At least they weren't moving from place to place.

"Did you see this in yesterday's newspaper?" she asked while holding out to me the ad for the talent show.

"O, yes!" I seized upon it. "May I keep this clipping?"

"Sure. I cut it out for you."

"I wanted to cut it out of the paper, but my mother never left the room and—well—I didn't want to discuss it with her last night."

"Lindy," she urged, "you really should get into it. You could win five dollars!"

"I'm thinking about it."

❋   ❋   ❋

Upon arriving home that afternoon, I found Mother in quite an exhilarated state. She had gone to see about the job, sub-zero temperatures notwithstanding.

"I think I made a favorable impression," she said, smiling broadly. "I probably have as much chance as any."

"Gee, Ma! That's good," I said. I didn't want to dampen her resolve, but I had never been separated from her before. The thought of it gave me a hollow, gnawing feeling in my chest. "How long before you'll know?"

"Well, they need someone right away, but there were so many applicants to screen through—you can imagine! It might take a week. I told them I'd need to give notice to the landlord here."

"Have you talked to Aunt Belle yet about my staying with them?"

"Well, I found the ad while I was there yesterday helping them move. They know I planned to look into it today."

"Do they have room for me?"

"Well,—"

She seemed uncertain.

"There's a daybed in the living room and a large closet off the dining room which was intended for dishes and linens, I guess—a kind of 'butler's pantry'—I've heard them called. Surely Aunt Belle doesn't own enough to fill all that space."

"A daybed? In the living room?"

"Yeah," Mother answered. "It won't be any different from here."

She was right, of course. I didn't find the idea very appealing, but we had to be practical. And it was closer to school.

The pay phone in the hall rang as we talked. The stout lady in Apartment 4, Mrs. Higgins, answered as she always did.

"I suppose we can work it out," I said resignedly.

Mrs. Higgins shouted through the door as she rapped. "Mrs. Albright!. Telephone for you!"

Mother opened the door. Mrs. Higgins wore a cotton print house dress.

"It's a *man*," Mrs. Higgins said, somehow giving the fact great import.

Mother ran down the hall as if commanded. I knew it was Harve, and I wondered what effect his return might have on the plans which were emerging as a result of his absence.

"It was Harve," Mother announced happily as she closed the door behind her. "He's back in town. He's going to pick me up in half an hour. We're going to go somewhere and talk."

"Okay," I said dismally.

"Are you all right?" she asked. "You'll be okay here, won't you?"

"Sure. Go ahead. I have some reading to do."

She leaned over me and kissed me as I sat on the sofa. "You poor kid," she said. "It's a helluva life," and proceeded to get ready for her date.

I turned the dial on the table radio looking for some music to read by while she pawed through the closet. "Sure wish I had something new to wear for a change," I heard her mumble as she found her patent leather pumps.

I settled onto the sofa with the biography I had taken from the school library for a book report. As I opened it, the newspaper clipping Marjorie had given me fell into my lap. Picking it up, I went to the open bathroom door where Mother was standing in front of the mirror in a black slip. She had plugged a long extension cord into a wall socket in the living room and was now curling the ends of her hair.

"I'm planning to audition for a talent contest at the Grayce

Theater," I said.

"Talent contest? I haven't heard anything about it."

"Auditions will be held Saturday morning and the contest will be Saturday night."

"What are you going to do?"

"Sing."

"Sing?" She snared another lock of dark hair and rolled it up in the curling iron. "What's the prize?"

"Five dollars."

"Five Dollars?" Another dark lock was trapped in the hot jaws of the curling iron. "Worth going after, I suppose. Do you think you sing well enough?"

Having pulled off a couple of successful coups during the past week, a date with Matt, and significant progress in mastering the blades—to say nothing of asserting myself in getting out of helping Aunt Belle move—I was riding a crest of self-confidence. "Yes, I do."

"Saturday morning? You know there's work to do here on Saturday morning."

"Can't it be done some other time?"

She pulled the curling-iron plug from the extension cord and proceeded to apply her makeup. There was no answer.

"Well?" I prodded.

After another moment of silence, she said, "I don't like the way we've been clashing lately. I really don't know whether to allow this or not. Give me some time to think about it."

"Mother! What harm can there be in it? And I stand as good a chance as any to walk away with the prize."

"It's just that I don't think it's a good policy to walk away from responsibility for some 'pie-in-the-sky' delusion."

"Five dollars is a delusion?"

"Sweetheart," she said, abandoning the discussion, "I'm getting ready to go out for the evening. I'm really not in the mood to argue with you right now. I've asked for some time to think about it. Can you give me that?"

She wiggled into her "little black dress" and proceeded to snap up the side seam. She had darkened her brows and lashes. Her lipstick was bright red, her hair shining. I fumed as I watched her cross the room to the dresser and rummage in her jewelry box. She hung around her neck almost the only piece of jewelry I had ever seen her wear—a gold chain from which a large black-onyx signet ring dangled.

"This is too dark to wear with a black dress," she complained. Removing it, she selected instead a rope of red beads and fastened matching earrings in place.

"Okay," I said. I would give her time to think about it, but *I would go!*

The doorbell rang as she rubbed a drop of perfume between her wrists. She pushed the buzzer releasing the lock on the lower door and took her new fur coat from the closet while waiting for Harve to appear.

"Hi," he said in his gravel voice as he stepped inside. Not quite blond, Harve was a man of average height and build who had gained a few pounds since his youth. He smelled of shaving lotion with strong undertones of nicotine and liquor. If he was distinctive in anything, it was that he was distinctive in nothing.

He took Mother's coat from her and held it as she slid into it. I never could understand what attraction he held for Mother, but I supposed I had no right to be critical. It wasn't really his fault he was not as tall as Matt. Maybe Matt would be pudgy, too, someday.

Matt pudgy? The thought amused me. I chuckled. Harve was not amused. He smoothed his blond mustache.

"'Miss America' finds me amusing," he said accusingly to Mother. Mother looked sternly at me.

"Please, Harve." Her tone was patronizing. It disgusted me. "I'm sure Lindy meant no harm."

"She's flying pretty high," he said. "Maybe her name has gone to her head," alluding to Colonel Lindbergh, the national idol of the moment.

Mother pretended not to hear. "We'll be going now, Dear," she said to me.

They were mumbling to each other in the hall after the door closed. I made myself comfortable on the sofa and opened to the title page of *The Life and Work of Susan B. Anthony,* by *Ida Husted Harper, (1898).* My eyes had scanned several pages before I realized that I had not remembered a single word. The pent up anger within me made it impossible to concentrate. To think I was obligated to that repulsive little man for my new coat--for the very roof over my head!

I got up from the sofa and found my boots. Bundled up in a coat, scarf and cap, I pulled my warm mittens off the shelf. Getting hotter and angrier every minute, I pawed through the clutter on the chest-of-drawers, finally locating the key under an envelope. Locking the door behind me, I made my way out into the night.

I ran--slowly at first--then faster--faster. My heart raced to keep pace; then settled into a deep, thrusting rhythm. I felt my rib cage expand and contract. As I took in great drafts of fresh air, I began to feel joy in the response of my body. A feeling of intoxication came over me. I became invincible. Arriving at an intersection, I casually looked both ways, then sprawled headlong over the fender of a car which came from behind and made a right turn right in front of me. I heard the brakes squeal. I bounced off and rolled back toward the curb.

I lay for a moment, stunned. Before I could respond to what happened, there were two dark faces looking into mine: one, a young man with a very black mustache. He wore no hat. His black hair shone sleek and shiny in the pale glow of the street light. Then a young woman appeared wearing a colorful scarf over her head and tied beneath her chin. Her brows were drawn together, her parted lips revealed straight, white teeth as she peered down into my face.

"You okay?" the man asked.

I couldn't answer.

"My God!" the woman exclaimed. Then looking at her companion, she spoke very rapidly in a foreign language—Spanish, I thought.

The man nodded. He went to the car and came back with a canvas tarpaulin, the kind painters and plasterers use. I didn't want them to cover me with it. It was stiff and stained. I attempted to sit up, but the scene spun before my eyes.

"Lay down!" the woman ordered. They covered me with the tarpaulin. "He's going to call an ambulance. Just be still a few minutes."

An ambulance!

The young man left.

I was glad for the tarpaulin. It was warm.

After what seemed an interminable time, he came back to where we waited.

"They're coming," he said. "How you feel?"

"Don't feel anything," I said.

They were the first words I had spoken. The young man and the young woman looked at each other. Relief was written on their faces.

We waited. I thought of Mother and Harve coming back to the apartment and finding me gone. They wouldn't even know where to look for me. I began to stir.

The woman shivered.

"Go wait in the car," the young man suggested to her.

"No, I wait," she answered.

"I think I'll be all right now," I said, again trying to sit up.

"No! no!" the young man said. He took the scarf from around his neck, folded it neatly and placed it on the pavement. Then, he gently urged me to lie down as he arranged it beneath my head.

"Were you running from somebody?" the woman asked.

I thought about that a moment. I guessed I was, but I said, "No. Just running."

"Just for fun?"

We heard the sirens. People began to gather. Such a fuss! I was all right.

"You go with her," the man instructed the woman. "I bring the car."

Inside the ambulance, a police officer questioned me, asked for my name and address. I asked him to please notify my mother of my whereabouts as soon as she got home. I thought about the distress an officer's presence would cause Harve, having just got out of a Cleveland jail, and I was almost amused.

As the ambulance raced through the intersections, sirens screaming, the young woman held my hand.

"What's your name?" she asked.

"Lindy," I replied absently. My mind was busy with what was going to happen now.

"Lindy? Very pretty name." she said, sincere concern showing in her face. "My name is Gloria."

I visualized being undressed and examined at the hospital. Naked, among strangers. Tears began to fill my eyes. "Will you stay with me, Gloria?" I begged.

"I will try." She squeezed my hand. "If they will allow me, I will stay."

With that assurance, I closed my eyes, suddenly very drowsy. The next thing I remember is being awakened by a nurse.

"Where am I?" I asked

"You're on an examining table at Johnson Emergency Hospital."

"Am I all right?"

"No broken bones. You took quite a bump on the head, but your thick cap helped. It could have been much worse."

"Did anybody call my mother?"

At that moment, I heard her voice.

They rolled my gurney out into the hall.

"Lindy! What happened?" I heard despair in her voice as she looked at me clad in a hospital gown.

Just then a young man in a white jacket appeared, the physician on duty, I assumed.

"You're her mother?"

"Yes."

"We're going to keep her overnight, just to check her vital signs from time to time. She has no broken bones, but she took a blow to the head when she fell. We expect everything to be fine. If so, she can leave in the morning."

"Shall I stay with her?" Mother asked.

"You may if you like." He shrugged. "I don't think it will be necessary."

They wheeled me into a ward and moved me to a firm, high, sanitized bed. Mother followed, Harve close behind. This wasn't in the script. He didn't like it at all.

"Where's Gloria?" I asked.

"Gloria? Who's Gloria?"

"She came in with me. I want to thank her."

"What does she look like?" Harve asked. "I'll see if I can find her. Maybe she's waiting out in the hall somewhere."

"She's dark--Spanish--wearing a bright headscarf."

She appeared in the doorway.

"There she is!" I exclaimed.

She came toward the bed. The young man waited in the doorway.

"This is your mother and father?" she asked.

"My mother."

"We still don't know what happened," Mother questioned.

"It was an accident. She was running. She ran into the car. We were turning. She ran--she bumped the fender and fell off."

"Where?" Mother asked.

"On thirty-fifth, I think." She turned to the young man. "It was thirty-fifth?"

He nodded. "Thirty-fifth and Pierce. The officer, he wrote it down." He gestured, moving his fingers across his left palm.

"This is my brother," Gloria explained.

The doctor entered the room. "I must ask you to leave the room.

You may continue your discussion in the hall."

I was relieved. I didn't know what to expect of Mother and Harve. Gloria and her brother had been so nice to me, and it really had not been their fault. I heard them with the officer in the hall.

I didn't sleep much that night. Every time I got into a deep sleep, the nurse was beside me, checking my pulse and blood pressure. The doctor came with a flash light and checked my pupils.

"Everything's okay so far," he assured me. He was a pleasant young man with dark-rimmed glasses.

They brought me orange juice, toast and tea the next morning. Then they brought my clothes. Among them was Gloria's brother's scarf. I laid it beside my coat and waited for Mother. She arrived at about nine o'clock.

"Do you feel well enough to ride the streetcar?" she asked.

"I feel okay, I guess."

"What's that?" she asked, noting the unfamiliar scarf.

"That's Gloria's brother's scarf," I said. "He folded it up and put it under my head last night when I was lying in the street waiting for the ambulance. I want to give it back to him."

This graphic portrayal of the accident shocked my mother. She turned pale. She took my arm tenderly as we walked out into the hall, scrutinizng me all the while. Then she led me to a chair.

"I'm going to call a cab," she announced.

Chapter 8

How Mother managed to get that job in the face of all that competition, I have never understood. True, she had graduated from high school in an era when a high school education was extraordinary. What's more, she had attended the Normal School for a year and had earned a *Teacher's Certificate* before I intruded into her life making of her an unwed mother.

Still, it was a time when the newspapers were full of reports of bank failures—even the Bank of the United States had failed at Christmastime last year—and every kind of business had had to discharge employees. How a private school for girls managed to exist was difficult to understand. Uncle Frank had some theories about it not being "*what* you know but *who* you know" that exempted some people from hardship.

Harve, thinking he saw an opportunity for me to get some money out of the accident, had obtained the names and addresses of Gloria and her brother, Joe Ruiz, from the police officer.

"You should sue," he advised Mother and me. "You're not rich, you know. It doesn't hurt a woman to have a little money of her own," he said to me. "You might want to go to college one of these days."

"I wouldn't have any idea of how to go about it," Mother said.

"Get a lawyer!"

"I can't afford a lawyer," Mother protested.

"Did you ask if they have any insurance?" I asked Harve. We had been discussing various types of insurance in *Business Training*.

"No, I didn't," he admitted.

"What's their address?"

He produced a notebook from his inside jacket pocket. "Here it is."

I took it from him and copied the information.

"What are you going to do?" he asked.

"I'm going to call 'em up—*if* they have a phone—which they prob'bly don't. This is not a very fashionable address. *Then* I'll arrange to take Joe's scarf back. *Then* maybe I can find out if they have any insurance."

For an instant, I thought I saw a look of respect come over Harve's face.

I had gone to the audition at the Grayce, with Mother's permission, granted without too much enthusiasm, and had won three dollars taking second place in the contest. First place went to an amateur magician who fascinated the audience performing sleight-of-hand tricks.

March 1, moving day, fell on Sunday in 1931. We had rented the apartment furnished so we had only our personal possessions to move. Harve's Essex had a trunk on the back, and by three of us crowding into the front seat, we could use the whole back seat for cartons of books, bed linens, towels, etcetera, which we had accumulated. I took the little study lamp to use at Aunt Belle's, and Mother took the table radio since a big console, property of the Trust Company, had been left behind for Aunt Belle and Uncle Frank. We were all packed up and waiting when Harve arrived.

Harve and I tolerated each other during the move, each grateful that we would be seeing little of each other from now on. He was not happy about Mother's taking a job. She thought it was because he cared for her, but I thought he feared losing control of her. She would no longer be available every time he called. And she would have her own money.

Arriving at Aunt Belle's, we now went around to the back door where we found Aunt Belle and Uncle Frank comfortable in their new quarters. The big, sun-drenched kitchen was fragrant with Aunt Belle's cooking. A pot of spaghetti simmered on the six-burner double-oven gas range, (the largest range I had ever seen,) which occupied a corner of the room.

Harve and Uncle Frank brought in my things. Aunt Belle showed me the big closet with it's built-in drawers and shelves. "You can be our little girl for awhile," she said, hugging me.

I liked the big old house with its large rooms. Looking out through the long windows, I imagined a snow-covered countryside and wished I could have lived in it back when the surrounding area was rural. The high ceilings—the spaciousness—provided a feeling of freedom which I thoroughly enjoyed. Dinner was served before I finished putting my things in place.

"Did you see the headlines in this morning's paper?" Uncle Frank asked Harve.

"Haven't had time," Harve complained. "Been helping the ladies, here, get organized for moving."

Aunt Belle and I exchanged glances. I rolled my eyes.

"What's in the headlines?" Harve asked.

"Well," Uncle Frank went on, "on Friday, the Bureau here got a telegram that the veteran's bonus bill had been passed, and the headlines on this morning's paper say three thousand veterans have already applied right here. They expect to have two hundred thousand dollars in the mail by tomorrow."

"Sonofagun!" Harve exclaimed. "Where's that paper?"

"Let's have our dinner first," Aunt Belle suggested.

"Yeah," Uncle Frank agreed. "After dinner."

"Okay," Harve agreed, "let's eat."

I listened while the conversation transversed such topics as the food on the table, the weather, and Mother's feelings about stepping into her new position. Harve settled down and enjoyed his dinner.

No longer confined to the limitations of a portable oven, Aunt Belle had made an apple pie. She and Uncle Frank were now getting their rent free plus a small wage which they earned together, and Uncle Frank was still working the used car lot albeit without much success. The move into the larger apartment had had an uplifting effect on both Uncle Frank and Aunt Belle. They felt a little more in control of their lives.

Aunt Belle served the apple pie with pride. Its perfectly browned crust and cinnamon fragrance evoked admiring comments from all. Mother poured a second cup of coffee all around, after which Harve made a bee-line for the newspaper in the living room to read about the veterans' bonus.

"Shit!" Harve swore, marching back into the kitchen where we all still sat at table. His thick blond brows were drawn together in a scowl. He was flushed with anger. "This isn't a bonus at all. This is a *loan!*"

Uncle Frank had a complete vocabulary of profanity of his own, but he became uncomfortable when such language was used in the presence of women—especially me. "Watch your language," he quietly admonished Harve. "There's ladies present."

Mother's face turned red.

"I'm sorry, *ladies!*" Harve said with mock sincerity. "It's just that the purpose of the bonus when it was introduced was to compensate veterans for the difference in pay between those who went and laid in the mud—in the trenches—and those who stayed at home—and made all the money!" With a broad gesture, he slapped the newspaper against his palm. "It was never intended to be a loan!"

"Gee!" Uncle Frank shook his head. "I didn't know that. That's quite a different story, isn't it? I wonder who's responsible for that?"

"A *loan!*" Harve said again in disgust. "I wonder how much of it they'll ever get back."

Aunt Belle started clearing the table. Mother and I got up to help. The men drifted into the living room still engaged in vehement discussion.

"Do you have to be at the dormitory by a certain time?" Aunt Belle asked Mother.

"I'd like to get settled before curfew."

"Curfew?"

"Yes. The students have to be in by ten."

"When will you have some time off?" I asked.

"One afternoon a week—Thursday—and major holidays when the girls all go home—such as Christmas vacation. I don't have to be there if everybody's gone."

That doesn't leave much time for me, I thought. I felt the corners of my mouth droop. My eyes filled with tears. I sniffed. I looked at Mother. She was crying, too. Suddenly we were in each other's arms. The tears flowed freely.

Aunt Belle found a handkerchief in her apron pocket, wiped her eyes and blew her nose. With pot holders, she carried the boiling teakettle to the sink and filled the dishpan.

"Come on, now," she said, bringing us both to terms with reality. "It's not a permanent separation. You'll be in the same town, and you can phone each other anytime."

"Sure," I said, already overwhelmed by loneliness even with Mother still in the same room with me.

"That's right," Mother agreed.

Occupying ourselves with the job at hand had a soothing effect on all of us. After the last dish was in place, we, too, wandered into the living room.

"Who d'ya think the Democrats will put up for president?" we heard Uncle Frank ask Harve.

"I don't think it makes much difference," Harve said. "I don't think Hoover will get elected again. The Dems can put up almost anybody they please and get him elected."

"I don't know about that. Al Smith is still mighty popular, even if he did lose in 1928."

"Yeah, but he's a 'wet.' If the country goes 'wet,' I'm out of a job."

"Can't people make a living selling booze legally?" Uncle Frank speculated.

"You mean open a saloon?" Harve asked. "That takes money, too. I don't have that much money."

"Rockefeller's been mentioned as a possibility for president."

"Why would he want the job?" Harve asked. "He's already the richest man in the country."

"Well, there's some talk about the Governor of New York as a candidate," Uncle Frank put in.

"Who's that? Is he a Democrat?"

"Yeah, he's a Democrat. Fella by the name of Roosevelt." He checked the paper again. "Franklin D. Roosevelt. They say he's a rich man—Harvard graduate—lawyer—former Assistant Secretary of the Navy under Wilson," he read aloud. "They say he's done some good things for the State of New York."

"Hmm," Harve said. "I don't know much about him—although I've heard of Theodore. O, *yes!*" he reflected, his memory refreshed, "Isn't he the delegate who swung himself to the podium on crutches and put Al Smith's name in nomination at the last convention?"

"Bygod!" Uncle Frank recalled, "I think you're right. I remember reading about it in the papers."

"Why, he's a *cripple!*" Harve exclaimed. "How could he be president?"

"Doesn't seem to have stopped him up to now. He's Governor of New York. Better'n either of us has done so far."

"Harve," Mother interjected, "I'm afraid I'm going to have to get over to the dormitory now. Maybe you two can discuss politics another time?"

Seizing the opportunity to extricate himself from Uncle Frank's uncomfortable logic, Harve willingly lifted himself from his comfortable chair. "Okay," he agreed. Then turning back to Uncle Frank he commented, "What a choice!"

I drew a deep breath. The time had come. Harve held Mother's coat for her and Uncle Frank helped Harve with his.

We all stood around while they fastened their galoshes and arranged their scarves and gloves. Then they were at the door. Mother kissed Aunt Belle and hugged Uncle Frank, then turned to me. We embraced warmly again, but we didn't cry this time.

"Come on," Harve said impatiently. "You'll see her again next week."

I slipped my coat over my shoulders and, with them, walked out to the front of the house where the car was parked. My teeth chattered as I waited at the curb for the car to warm up, watching the exhaust billow into the crisp, cold air. After another kiss blown to the wind, they were gone.

I ran back into the house and hung up my coat. It was growing dark. With Mother gone, the living room seemed like a tomb.

Aunt Belle pulled the chain of the bridge lamp above her chair. The glowing bulb brought a measure of cheer and warmth into the depressed atmosphere. She leaned forward and turned on the big console radio.

"It's almost six o'clock," she announced as she paged through the thick Sunday newspaper. "There's a good show on WGN. 'Harbor Lights.' Want to hear it?"

"I s'pose," I said half-heartedly, hoping the diversion would lift my spirits.

"We interrupt this program to bring you the following announcement," a sonorous voice from the big brown box declared ominously. *Charles A. Lindbergh, Jr., twenty-month-old infant son of Col. Charles A. Lindbergh and Anne Morrow Lindbergh, is missing from his crib in the family home in Hopewell, New Jersey. It is feared he has been kidnapped."*

Chapter 9

A new pattern evolved. Mother had dinner with us every Thursday evening. Sometimes Harve joined us, other times he came later in the evening unless he happened to be out of town.

I now walked to school unless the weather was inclement, and had made some new acquaintances along the way. I continued to see Matt on weekends, and sometimes had Sunday-night supper with his family.

Matt lived in a rambling old farmhouse which had been his grandfather's. When the city began to crowd the boundaries of the farm, it became profitable to subdivide the land and allow the city to develop around the big old house.

Matt's father, Cyrus, a huge barrel-chested man well over six feet tall, was a motorman on the Rapid Transit line, which was as secure a position as could be found. His sisters, Annette and Marie, both younger than I, regarded me as somewhat peculiar because I lived so unconventionally. The attitude of Matt's mother was unmistakably one of pity.

Once, while in the kitchen helping to do the dishes after a

Sunday-night supper of sliced, cold roast beef and cheese sand-wiches, Matt's mother told me of his account of the apartment.

"Matt said the kitchen is behind two doors, and the bed folds up into the closet," she said in disbelief.

"Yes, that's true."

"What's the world coming to? How can people live like that?" she lamented plaintively.

"It's really quite convenient," I assured her. "Of course, it's intended for only two people—not for a family."

"But you don't live there any more."

"No, I share an apartment with my aunt and uncle now."

"And you have more room?"

"There is more living space, yes. The house was a mansion before it was divided into separate apartments. The rooms are large."

She shook her head.

"Tsk! tsk!" she said sorrowfully.

"Ma!" Annette said angrily to her mother. "Stop making her feel like a freak! Lindy is not unhappy just because she lives in a rooming house! Times have changed. People do what they have to do."

Mrs. Dorsey nodded and sighed.

❋　　❋　　❋

Matt graduated valedictorian in June of 1931, and made plans to go to State university on scholarships he had earned, one from State and another through his father's union affiliation.

Newspapers carried stories of the deepening depression around the country—the entire world. Corruption in high places was exposed almost daily ranging from misuse of funds which lead to the closing of banks, to the imprisonment for tax evasion of Al Capone, America's most notorious gangster.

Still, some amazing feats were being reported. They sustained our hopes and reminded us that a magical and limitless future lay ahead if we could but lick this paralyzing depression.

Wiley Post and Harold Gatty had taken off in a monoplane to

circumnavigate the globe in less than *nine days!* They had come back to crushing throngs of exuberant admirers who were still lionizing Lindbergh for his solo flight across the Atlantic just four years before.

❋　　❋　　❋

Violet and Bob located me through the manager of the Riverside Theater where I had appeared in another talent contest. A young Ukranian couple, they called me one evening to tell me they would like to meet me.

"I'm ever so pleased that you should invite me to sing at your wedding," I told them as we sat one Saturday afternoon in Aunt Belle's sunny living room.

"Well," the young couple squirmed uneasily, "we have someone to sing at the wedding. A relative of Bob's. She's expecting to be asked."

"I don't understand," I said. "What is it you want of me?"

"Some of our friends have put together a little orchestra--a concertina and a saxaphone and--what else?" She turned to her fiance. They held hands as they sat on the daybed.

"A drum," he added.

"But there is no vocalist," she continued. "We'd like to have you sing with the group for the dance after the wedding."

"What kind of music do they play?"

"Standard popular," the girl answered. "They might get some requests from the guests or our parents, but--

"Then they'll do their own singing," Bob interjected. He slapped his thigh and laughed in anticipation. He evidently knew both families well.

"Just sing what you know."

I knew the words and music to most of the popular songs.

"How does the group feel about your getting a vocalist for them? Usually the vocalist is decided by the group, isn't it?"

"They've been looking for someone," Violet said, turning to her fiance for confirmation. He nodded. "When we told them we heard you and liked your performance, they said we should go ahead and try to get hold of you."

"Well," I hesitated—

"We've allowed ten dollars for a vocalist," Violet said uncertainly. "We've been saving for a long time. Would that be enough?"

Ten dollars! I did my best to appear unruffled by such an exorbitant figure.

"Why, yes," I said with as much aplomb as I could marshal. "I guess that would be satisfactory. I would just like to meet the group and work with them before the wedding dance, if that can be arranged."

So began a long series of such engagements which continued after my high school graduation in 1932. A couple of weeks after I performed at Violet's wedding dance, I received a call from one of her friends who was also planning a wedding. Then another and another. During the months of May and June, I was busy every weekend.

Matt often accompanied me if he was in town. When I wasn't singing, we would dance or sit quietly and sip the wine that was so generously urged upon us by the Polish and Italian residents of the south side. By saving a portion of each year's legal allotment of homemade wine and beer for such special occasions, it was possible to accumulate enough for a large gathering. Besides, the larger extended family was always ready to contribute to a good cause.

These dances were usually held in church halls, much to the chagrin of Aunt Belle. An ardent Presbyterian, she neither drank nor danced.

"Disgraceful!" she would expostulate when afterward I would talk about the people I had met and the old world customs I had observed. She would sometimes quote the *Bible* about the dangers of "strong drink," whereupon Uncle Frank, who referred to himself as an *Innocent Bystander* in matters of religion, would remind her that, according to legend, the changing of water into wine at a wedding was the first miracle of Christ.

Poor Aunt Belle! She found the contradiction totally discombobulating. I had witnessed both kinds of celebrations and felt that the Polish and Italians had, by far, the most fun.

The taste of these beverages did not set well on my tongue. I found them bitter or sour and left more in the glass than I drank, except on one occasion when I was deceived by the innocent flavor of the juice of white grapes. Matt, too, had had more than just a polite sip.

We were leaving after my last song when Tony Kwiezinski, father of the bride, approached us with a tray. His narrow pants were cinched beneath his protruding abdomen giving the nervous impression that they were about to drop to his ankles at any moment. He was reinforced on his right by Gina, his plump wife. On the tray were two pieces of wedding cake, each wrapped in waxed paper, and two glasses of the fruity white wine.

"Have a glass of wine before you go," Tony invited. "Take the cake home. Enjoy it tomorrow."

Not wanting to offend, we accepted their hospitality. It was, indeed, good wine.

"You know," Gina confided, "they say if you sleep on a piece of wedding cake, you will dream of your future husband."

Tony evaluated Matt with raised eyebrows.

Whether because of the wine or the situation, I felt my cheeks flush. Matt, too, was uncomfortable.

Well past midnight, we were able to make a prudent departure. Matt didn't have the use of the car this evening, so we set out on foot leaving the cacophony of the party behind. In the contrasting silence, we slowed our pace and inhaled the perfume of the balmy June night. Past darkened windows of clapboard flats and cottages we strolled, our moist hands clasped; past clipped hedges and low iron fences where little gates hung open, forgotten by the owners of dolls and tricycles, awaiting a new day. Except for rustliing treetops, where a light breeze danced, the city was silent around us.

In the shadow of a huge old chestnut tree where blossoms

strewed the sidewalk, Matt drew me to him and kissed me seductively. We held each other for a long moment, then strolled wordlessly, the hunger for each other shouting down every admonition, every plea, every impediment to fulfillment.

Where a single streetlight swung above the intersections, we assumed nonchallance and crossed sedately, seeking—always seeking—the islands of shadow which dotted the path ahead where we could secretly embrace and again explore each other's contours. Block after block we walked in the summer night, touching, tasting, inhaling each other—until at last we were back at the rooming house on National Avenue.

Loitering at the back door, hand in hand, we walked past the stoop to the darkness behind the house. There we sank to the soft carpet of grass in the shadow of the board fence which separated the back yard from the used car lot. Unwilling to relinquish even a moment of this gentle night, we clung to each other.

His hair was soft on my fingers as I cradled his head. The sweet clover emitted its distinctive scent as it cushioned our eager bodies. Warm breezes played on our skin where our hands found ever more-enticing smoothness to caress and fondle as barriers to intimacy were discarded, one by one.

The drumbeat within my chest intoned a hypnotic chant. In a state of trance, still acutely aware, I welcomed Matt with joyous disbelief. Amid skyrockets and wildly ringing bells, I heard him breathe, "Omigod, Lindy! How long I've wanted you!"

Emerging at last into silence, I noted the sky growing pink.

"Matt! Matt!" I whispered. "You'd better be going home."

"Yeah," he rasped.

It was the dawn of a new day.

☙❧

Chapter 10

While the sensuous young swayed to *How Deep is the Ocean*, the jobless thousands lamented to the tune of *Brother, Can You Spare a Dime?* They could be found around fires at the edges of towns and at the back doors of restaurants looking for food. Soup kitchens, funded by local governments and charities, fed hundreds daily.

In June, a contingent of World War veterans joined a thousand who preceded them in a march on Washington, D.C.. From farms and cities across the nation, they had come, bonus certificates in hand, demanding the promised cash. They occupied vacant federal buildings which were scheduled to be razed, and spilled over into encampments where they lived in tents and packing crates. It was reported that twenty thousand occupied the Marks Flats west of the Capitol near Third and Pennsylvania Avenues, while an even larger number camped on the Anacostia Flats on the south bank of the Anacostia River.

Becoming surly and unruly, they had refused to comply with police demands that they move out. Fighting broke out between the veterans and police on numerous occasions.

"Dammit, Frank!" Harve railed, red-faced with anger, "These guys are not all criminals and communists like the government is trying to make us believe. They're veterans. Guys who love their country. Guys who were hailed at the end of the war--for 'making the world safe for democracy' --Wilson told us. They walked--hitchiked--rode the rods from all over the country to come together for this demonstration."

"It's a damned shame, I know," Uncle Frank commiserated. He was hesitant to do anything but agree with Harve, since he, himself, had been excused from military service for some reason which was never clear to me.

❋ ❋ ❋

"How do you feel about caps and gowns?" I asked Marjorie as we walked toward Assembly B. All candidates for graduation had been summoned by intercom to vote.

"I had instructions from my folks to vote against it," Marjorie confided. "I don't really care too much. I think caps and gowns should be reserved for college, don't you?"

"Yes," I agreed, "but a lot of these kids will never see the inside of a college. They feel they deserve this as a kind of reward."

"Did you deposit for the annual?"

"Yes, but there weren't enough of us. We all got our fifty cents back."

"I felt lucky to subscribe to the *Cardinal.* I kept my copies. Those weeklies will have to be my annual--the only remembrance I'll have."

"I didn't have the foresight to do even that," I admitted.

"No prom either, eh?"

"Nope. Well--some other life, maybe."

We both chuckled as we took our seats.

❋ ❋ ❋

There would be no caps and gowns for *this* class. Feelings ran high, but when hands were raised and counted, the *nays* overruled the *yeas* by a substantial majority. The mourning sounds of weeping filled the halls as we were dismissed. Girls flocked to the washrooms where they sobbed in each other's arms. Some of the boys stood in knots, here and there, their red-rimmed eyes betraying their manly equanimity.

I considered myself lucky to have a new dress—final project of my sewing class, the last stitches taken minutes before putting it on the very evening of the graduation ceremony. Boys wore suits if they were lucky enough to own one. Some were borrowed—here one a little tight across the shoulders—there another a little long at the cuff. While *Pomp and Circumstance* filled Assembly A, we marched two abreast down the outer aisles past parents who sat, two to a seat, behind the adult-size school desks which filled the room.

In Washington, the veterans obstinately held their ground throughout the heat of summer, confident that no soldier would go into action against them. The standoff reached a crisis at the end of July when President Hoover called on General Douglas MacArthur to lead United States Army troops into the fracas. On July 29, the newspapers spread pages of pictures and reported that twenty steel-helmeted soldiers led the way, revolvers drawn, followed by cavalry, bayonets and tanks.

Scrambling with whatever possessions they could salvage, the veterans set fire to the encampments. Despite the summer heat, residents in the area were forced to close their windows and doors against the heavy barrage of tear gas and smoke. One veteran and one policeman lost their lives. Thus General MacArthur succeeded in routing the veterans from the skeletal buildings and shack villages.

The nation was appalled. Harve was both enraged and heartbroken. He did not need the money promised by the bonus. He was making lots of money, but he was breaking the law to do it which was essentially against his nature. He had fought for his country, which he loved. He seemed confused, his whole value structure contorted as a building twisted by a tornado. For the first time, I felt sympathy for him and realized there were thousands like him.

The summer of '32 was a paradox. Everything *seemed* the same, yet everything was different. The milkman's horse could be heard clop-clopping at the same hour every morning, his bottles tinkling in their wire baskets. True to tradition, the mailman walked his route in all kinds of weather, and the newsboy served his customers faithfully, but the economy languished. A subliminal tension could be felt as the nation waited for something to happen.

Radios were now almost everywhere. They told us that unemployment had reached twenty-four per cent; that General MacArthur, in a commencement speech, warned that "undefended riches provoke war," and called for a stronger defense; while President Hoover asked for sweeping arms cuts worldwide.

Symphonies and operas were canceled for the season for lack of funding, while Louis Armstrong, with his orchestra, made his first trip abroad. Jack Benny made his debut on the network and the lines at the soup kitchens grew longer and longer.

To earn enough to supplement his scholarships and return to the university in the fall, Matt worked part-time for a couple of neighborhood grocers who were eager to help a young man in his quest of a college education. He stocked shelves, waited on trade, swept sidewalks and sometimes drove a small truck delivering grocery orders, most of which were bought on credit. "I don't know how much longer Otto can stay in business," he once said as we strolled toward the park. "His creditors are after their money, and Otto hasn't the heart to put pressure on his customers."

"Gee! What can a person do in a situation like that? Isn't there some way—through the courts maybe—that a person can collect what he's got coming? I mean—they can't expect the grocer to support 'em out of his own pocket, can they?"

"The point is they don't have anything left anymore. Most of 'em have lost the homes they're living in and are just living out the equity."

"What's 'equity,' Matt?"

"*Equity?*"

He seemed appalled by my ignorance—the ignorance endemic to poverty.

"'Equity' represents the amount of money they've already paid—the degree of ownership. It gets kind of complicated," he explained.

"Every case is different. Anyway, the county won't help 'em until their degree of ownership--their equity--is nil. All used up."

"How do you know all these things, Matt?"

"Because we talk about them at the dinner table--my dad and my brother and I."

"How's your dad doing?"

"Dad's in pretty good shape. He owns the house outright-- inherited it from my grandparents. We moved in to help Grandma and to take care of the place after Grandpa died, and so far, Dad's job seems safe. Of course, taxes are going to go up with so many people on relief. If the Rapid Transit should go bankrupt--"

"What would happen then?"

"Well," he mused, " I expect we'd all have to pull together. You know," he changed his tack, "you read about the twenty-four or -five per cent unemployed, but that leaves seventy-five per cent em- ployed. I just don't think it'll get that bad."

His optimistic outlook was so different, my spirits were refreshed.

✼   ✼   ✼

I had made several attempts to locate Gloria and her brother Joe Ruiz. The telephone directory yielded nothing, neither did the information operator. Our moving shortly after the accident may have accounted for their inability to contact me, if, indeed, they ever tried.

Harve was sure they would keep their distance out of fear of a law suit. I was sure they just didn't have anything. I was fine, apparently. The matter waned.

One bright note was that I was not pregnant, a fact for which both Matt and I felt ourselves immensely lucky. A pregnancy at this time would have been catastrophic to Matt's future and mine as well.

I continued to sing at weddings and neighborhood theaters on talent nights always coming away with a few more dollars than I expected. People needed entertainment, and the possibility of a bonanza on Bank Night at neighborhood movie theaters drew crowds with their quarters and coupons.

Mother had dinner with us every Thursday evening, bringing a grocery bag full of treats for the table. Harve would always pick her up at about eight-thirty. He hadn't had any more brushes with the law although he was presumably still bootlegging. On these occasions, the two men would resume their spirited discussions about the political scene. Harve had not forgotten Uncle Frank's put-down during a previous conversation.

"Looks as though you might not be in business too much longer," Uncle Frank observed one evening as we all sat in the living room.

"You think not?" Harve parried.

"The Volstead Act is on the way out."

"That depends on who gets elected," Harve countered.

"Not any more. Even Hoover is for revocation now."

"Yeah, that's what I've been reading." Harve conceded   " A little late to make a difference in the election, wouldn't you say?"

"Never can tell," Uncle Frank speculated. "They've got a lot of good ideas lately, like cutting their own salaries. It   may   help, maybe not. "

"Well, I guess it had to come," Harve conceded.

"What had to come?"

"Repeal."

Surprised by Harve's easy concession, as we all were, Uncle Frank asked, "How's that?"

"The word is the government is filing tax liens against bootleg distillers."

"Can they do that?" I asked.

"Sure can." He seemed surprised that I had been listening.

"How?" Mother asked.

"They can subpoena the records," Harve informed us authoritatively.

"If there are any," I speculated.

"That's right. If there are any. They have to have some records. How would they split the take?"

"You've got some plans, I take it," Uncle Frank surmised, addressing Harve.

"Yup! I might throw in my lot with a customer of mine and go legit."

"You mean go into the *saloon* business?" Mother asked. Her tone was derogatory.

"Nope. A supper club, maybe. Something with class—like the *Cotton Club* in Harlem—or the *Copa Cabana*.

"Where?" Mother wanted to know. "Here in town?"

"Probably. We're just tossing the idea around right now. Nothing is definite. We'll wait and see what this election brings."

"Yeah," Aunt Belle piped. "I wonder who the Democrats are going to put up." She rolled up a pair of Uncle Frank's socks she'd been darning and placed it, like an egg in a nest, among others which lay beside her on the sofa.

Aunt Belle? Speaking out in a political discussion? The radio was transforming this sweet mouse—this dry Presbyterian—into someone with an interest in the world beyond the kitchen. We were all a little surprised—and amused.

"What do any of you know about John Garner?" she asked. "I've been hearing his name in the news a lot."

"Who's John Garner?" I asked. "I never heard of him."

"Neither have I. That's why I asked."

"'Cactus Jack?' He's from Texas, I know," Harve obliged.

"He's Speaker of the House. Been in Congress for thirty years," Uncle Frank told us. It disgusted him that we didn't know that. "He's been a fine legislator. Has a big constituency. Lots of people are for him. Think he'd make a fine president."

"I'm for Roosevelt," I announced.

"Why? Because he's good-looking?" Harve asked.

"No—although he *is* good-looking." To hear him, a person might think I didn't have a brain in my head. "I've been reading about some of the things he's done for the unemployed in the State of New York—like the temporary relief act he put through the state legislature."

Harve smiled at Uncle Frank. "First thing you know, *they'll* be telling *us* how to vote," he quipped with a nod of his head in our direction.

"Hell!" Uncle Frank exclaimed. "Why not? The men haven't done so well up to now. Just look at this country!"

There was a hint of new respect in the way Harve regarded all of us women. "Maybe you're right," he admitted. Then, looking ahead, he said, "I sure as hell would like to be at that convention next week."

"It's going to be broadcast on the network," Aunt Belle informed us. "I'm going to listen to every minute of it."

"Me, too," I added. "Whenever I can."

"You can't vote yet, Honey," Uncle Frank told me.

"I know. I think it's unfair to make us wait until we're twenty-one. As if we didn't have any brains." I sulked.

"Next time," they assured me. "You'll be twenty-two."

"Yeah," I leered. "Next time!"

عراق

Chapter 11

We hurried to finish our chores so we could take up our most comfortable positions in the living room around the big console radio. The convention that year was in Chicago, not too many miles away, but we were enthralled by the proximity we felt to that body of elected delegates who might, by sheer force of will, bring forth a savior from among the candidates to rescue us from the gray misery of recent years.

As the convention got under way, more and more of the upstairs tenants found a reason to use the back stairway, bringing them into the lower hall which exited to the outside. From the hall, they could look into the kitchen on one side and the dining-living room on the other. There they lingered in the doorway, sometimes sitting on the steps, listening, until Aunt Belle invited them to come inside where they gingerly seated themselves, taking in every word.

There was Erma and John Edwards, a couple in their late forties, whose youthful dreams of security by dint of sheer industry and thrift lay comatose behind their pale blue eyes. They lived in Apartment 7, two rooms right above our kitchen. They had no radio of their own and were appropriately impressed by the miracle of hearing every word from Chicago "as if you're in the same room."

Jewel and her mother, Maggie Alderson, occupied Apartment 6, a single sleeping room with a two-burner gas plate, their only closet a pegged board screwed to the wall. Two beautiful faces with smooth, milk-white skin~lots of skin~to cover their enormous, misshapen bodies. Their loud arguments were often heard in the hall and down the stairs, and they were sometimes seen with swollen faces and bruises on their fleshy arms. Winter was especially hard for them since they were almost prisoners in their small quarters, their huge bodies having virtually immobilized them.

Each afternoon during the convention, they lumbered down the stairs which groaned under their combined weight. They were happy to have a place to go. Uncle Frank confided to Aunt Belle his concern that the old stairway might collapse, and thought he might speak to them about using it one at a time. But Aunt Belle was shocked and angered by the suggestion, so he said nothing.

Day after day they sat, through all the days and evenings of the convention, in freshly-ironed cotton dresses. Washed, combed and lipsticked, they sedately occupied the entire daybed they sat upon so that Aunt Belle was obliged to arrange the dining-room chairs to provide seating for everyone.

As the hours and days went by, the shy visitors became acquainted with each other. Stan Witkowski, a loner, about forty-five, who lived in Apartment 5, brought a bag of mixed candy. He hired out by the day as a mechanic and was employed more often than not.

Not to be outdone, the Alderson ladies contributed a sackful of popcorn. The next day Mrs. Edwards served a plate of cookies carefully produced from ingredients provided by the County.

Aunt Belle sat at the diningroom table with a pencil. Before her was a sheet of grey stationery with a silver deckle edge, removed for this special occasion from a box she had received for Christmas several years before. On it she kept a record of the votes from each state for each candidate. This little exercise served to heighten the tension among the listeners. Occasionally someone would leave his chair to view the figures.

"I thought Al Smith would do better'n that," Stan remarked after looking over Aunt Belle's shoulder.

"It's early," Uncle Frank observed. "He may pick up more votes on the second ballot."

"Roosevelt's got a majority," Mr. Edwards noted. "Six hundred sixty-six and a quarter votes."

"Not enough," I said. "He needs two-thirds."

"It could still go to Garner when they take another ballot," Uncle Frank commented.

By Friday, the tenants, who heretofore had passed each other in the hall like strangers, were well acquainted.

"They've already taken three ballots," Jewel noted. "I never knew selecting a candidate was so complicated."

"What *did* you think?" Stan asked her.

"I guess I never thought about it at all," she admitted.

"A-L-A-A-S-S-S-K-A-H-!" shouted the radio.

"Gonna vote?"

"We're not registered."

"Well, get registered," Stan ordered.

"How do you do that?" Maggie asked.

"You go down to City Hall and tell 'em you want to register to vote. They'll tell you where to go and what to do."

"A-R-I-Z-O-O-N-N-N-A-H-!" the chairman called.

Jewel and her mother exchanged glances. That would require a trip downtown.

"Don't waste any time," Stan cautioned them. "Do it before the cold weather comes. It don't cost nothin' but ten cents for car fare."

Aunt Belle smiled to herself as she listened and made her tabulations.

"C-A-A-L-L-I-F-O-R-R-N-N-I-A-A-H!-!-!"

There was a pause. We fell silent as a low rumble rippled through the convention hall. California had been a staunch holdout for "Cactus Jack" Garner. The rumble grew to a low roar. The chairman's gavel was heard again.

"MR. McADOO! MAY WE HEAR FROM CALIFORNIA

PLEASE?"

"Who is McAdoo?" Aunt Belle asked nobody in particular.

A glimmer of remembrance appeared in Mr. Edwards' eyes. "I wonder if that's the same McAdoo who lost the nomination in 1924 because of the two-thirds rule?"

"Sure is!" Uncle Frank leaned forward in his chair—"Wilson's son-in-law." The radio, like a living person in the room, again demanded our attention.

"MR. CHAIR-M-A-A-H-N!"

The gavel banged. The background noise subsided.

"MR. CHAIR-M-A-A-H-N, CALIFORNIA CAME HERE TO NOM-INATE A PRESIDENT OF THE UNITED STATES. SHE DID NOT COME TO DEADLOCK THE CONVENTION. . . . CALIFORNIA CASTS FORTY-FOUR VOTES FOR FRANKLIN D. ROOSEVELT."

The roar was electrifying. An announcer described the pandemonium. A demonstration erupted in the convention hall—the elated FDR supporters snaking through and around the hall, waving signs while the band played *Happy Days Are Here Again* over and over. I felt prickles at the back of my neck.

Suddenly it was New Year's Eve at our house! Hugging, kissing and dancing went on in our living-dining room where almost the whole residency of the building was congregated.

From that point on, the states fell into line like dominoes. Listening, I felt that I had participated in this historic event. The very air seemed charged with hope. There were smiles all around this strangely unrelated group.

Aunt Belle left her tabulations and went into the kitchen. I followed. It was time to celebrate. She had baked a cake during the afternoon and was now filling the coffee pot.

When we came back into the room, we heard that Mr. Roosevelt would be *flying* to the convention from Albany—the wonder of it!—breaking a longstanding tradition of modestly accepting the nomination later, possibly the next day, with reporters and photographers gathered around his front porch. Roosevelt, himself, would address the convention before it adjourned the following day!

✻   ✻   ✻

The abnormally cool weather which had prevailed during the spring continued through the end of June. Saturday, the second day of July, found both Aunt Belle and me wearing sweaters. For the hundredth time, I heard her complain, "Is it ever going to warm up?"

Together, we washed the breakfast dishes. While she mopped the huge kitchen floor and the back hall, I dusted and vacuumed the other rooms. Serving snacks in the living and dining room and accommodating visitors over a period of days had left a feeling of stickiness and untidiness throughout. We knew they'd all be back tonight to hear Roosevelt give his acceptance speech.

Uncle Frank took on the cleaning of the reception area at the front of the building, the upper hall and the front and back stairs. With his long legs and strong arms, he made short work of it.

As evening descended, our visitors began to arrive. First to appear were the loneliest of all, the Aldersons. We had heard them earlier as they took baths, (there was hot water on Saturdays), and they appeared looking freshly groomed, in their starched, cotton print dresses.

Soon to follow was Stan. He was of average build, and dressed tonight in dark pants and a white shirt, open at the neck and with the cuffs turned up. His dark, curly hair was now showing some grey. Despite his rugged features, he was handsomer this evening than I had ever seen him. He carried a tall brown paper bag which he handed to Uncle Frank. In it were two unlabeled bottles of wine.

"Where'd you get these?" Uncle Frank asked with a wicked smile.

"My brother. It's homemade. Elderberry. I thought maybe—you know—afterwards—"

Uncle Frank smiled. "Sure! Thanks!" He carried them to the ice-box in the pantry.

Next came the Edwards, Mrs. Edwards in the lead, bearing a plate of cookies.

Finally, to my extreme pleasure, came Matt. He was wearing a light blue polo shirt with dark trousers and white shoes. The short sleeves exposed his downy, muscular arms and shiny gold graduation watch. I introduced him to the group with pride.

Matt placed two chairs for us at the far end of the dining room table, away from the group. As the radio crackled to life, we all sat rapt as if in church. We were told how the nominee, with his wife and family, had traveled by plane from Albany to Chicago, in very bad flying weather, in only seven hours!

Each of us had a stake in the future of one dimension or another. Since Matt and I were the youngest, our stake was the greatest. We paid attention.

It was an uplifted, though solemn group who heard Mr. Roosevelt say, at the end of his speech:

"I pledge you, I pledge myself, to a new deal, for the American people."

Matt and I stood in the doorway, hand in hand, as we listened to Roosevelt's final words. As we headed for the back door, I saw Aunt Belle and Uncle Frank turn toward the kitchen for the cookies and the wine.

Chapter 12

The euphoria following the nomination dissipated. Like drunks awaking with a hangover, we faced reality. The election still lay more than two months ahead and the inauguration four months beyond that.

A pale yellow leaf on the chevron brick walk flagged my attention as Matt and I returned from a date one Saturday night in August. It lay, as if by design, in a shaft of light from the used car lot which filtered through the leaves of the old maple tree in the front yard. I stooped to pick it up. As I caressed it with my fingers, it yielded its message: *Autumn lurks.*

Throughout the summer, we had, again and again, found the darkened area beside the board fence in the back yard. I sometimes wondered how much Aunt Belle and Uncle Frank knew—if they suspected our trysting place.

As we approached the house now, a myriad of unspoken uncertainties hung between us, an unseen barrier. Intimacy required privacy—craved comfort. We had none. Even tonight there was a chill in the air.

"How did you do this summer?" I asked, knowing he would soon be winding up his vacation jobs and heading back to the university.

"I managed to get enough together to go back," he answered.

I stroked the back of his neck as I sat a step above him on the front porch, while I twirled the yellow leaf between the thumb and forefinger of my other hand.

"This will be your second year."

"Yup."

"Have you decided what field you're going into?"

"Nope."

Silence. I tried again.

"Are you looking forward to going back?"

"Mm-hmm."

"I suppose you've made a lot of friends there."

"Mmm, yeah."

"You're not very talkative this evening."

He grunted. "Hmph!"

"Something on your mind?"

Silence again. Then, "Yeah, I guess so."

"Can you tell me?"

He nodded, withdrawing from my caressing fingers.

I withdrew my hand and waited. Evidently, my caresses were unwelcome tonight. The silent moments ticked off interminably.

"Lindy," he said, alerting me to what was to follow since I couldn't remember the last time he had used my name.

"Yes?"

"Lindy, I think it would be a good idea if we both dated other people for a while."

What's this? I felt my brows come together. He was alternately picking at a cuticle and studying the lines of his palm.

"We're both still so young," he went on. He had obviously given this speech a lot of thought. It was carefully rehearsed and gushing now. "It isn't as though you'd have any trouble finding another date. I've seen the guys drooling over you at these wedding dances. Maybe you should give yourself a chance. You might find some-body better than me—I—am."

I was numb. This was not the loving, caring Matt I knew. I remembered his mother's derogatory view of my lifestyle and detected overtones of someone outside of Matt. How did his sister,

Annette, refer to me in reprimanding her mother not long ago? A freak? "Stop making her feel like a freak," she had said. I felt now as I did after I fell off the fender of Ruiz' car and lay in the street with a concussion.

Somebody inside of me said, "Okay, Matt. If that's the way you want it—we'll try it for awhile."

He stood up then, and, taking my hand, pulled me up, too. We stood on the brick walk facing each other. Speckles of light from the car lot fell on his face as a breeze stirred the branches atop the big tree.

"Thanks, Lindy," he said. "I really think it will be better for both of us."

He took both of my hands in his and kissed me on the forehead. Then he stepped back. My hands fell to my sides. Quickly he turned and, with a determined step, walked toward the public sidewalk. In confused disbelief, I watched him stride past the car lot.

A lump rose in my throat, swelled and hardened. It hurt. The tears welled. I sat on the steps, arms folded across my knees, and sobbed into my elbow. Then, thinking I must not be found here by a tenant coming home, I went to the darkened spot in the back yard where we had made love so often, and released my grief.

Matt! Matt, whom I had trusted with my confidences, my love, my body; because of his intellect, because of his sportsmanship, because of his family—his background—his values. All the indicators had seemed so positive. What had I done wrong? We had both been virgin. Had I given more than he ?

❋   ❋   ❋

The used car lot gave Uncle Frank an escape from the house occasionally, but he couldn't spend all his time there lest other salesmen feel he was crowding them out. When he was at home, he was restless, playing solitaire, working crossword puzzles, jigsaw puzzles, reading the newspapers, pacing. I tried to interest him in a library card, but the library was beyond walking distance, and streetcar fare—well— Reading books was outside his sphere of interest which right now consisted solely of getting a job.

The big old house with its obscure, neglected corners became Aunt Belle's project—her career—her obsession. Never at a loss for something to do, she scrubbed, painted, made fresh and beautiful. She began to look upon Uncle Frank as a drone. The harder she worked and the more effective she was, the more guilt Uncle Frank felt. I could see that Aunt Belle was punishing him with his guilt as she worked even more diligently. Had she had anything to spend besides her energy, that old rooming house would have been restored to its original elegance.

I recall an incident wherein Uncle Frank, with a board across his lap, sat in the living room playing his continual solitaire while Aunt Belle ran a vacuum cleaner around his feet, expecting him to move. Instead, he simply raised his feet and continued snapping his cards. Aunt Belle became enraged. They barked at each other over the roar of the vacuum cleaner.

"Are you getting so lazy you can't even move to let a person clean?" she snarled.

"O, shut your face!" he snapped.

"Just *look* at that! Won't even move."

"You're getting pretty high and mighty around here, aren't you, little girl?" He knew the *little girl* would infuriate her.

"Why not?" she stormed at him. "Looks like I'm the one doing all the work around here."

"*Izzat so!* You forgot already, didn't you? All the coal I bale into that hungry beast down in the basement all winter long. And the tons of ashes I haul out! And the snow! Who shovels all the snow around here? And spreads ashes on the ice—so you won't fall on your little ass?"

"All right! All right! Calm down!"

These altercations left me quaking. I was much too young, too inexperienced to evaluate the seriousness of the petty quarrels which erupted now between Aunt Belle and Uncle Frank. My separation from Mother had been bearable only to the degree that Aunt Belle and Uncle Frank provided some stability. The shaky state of the economy, the prevailing attitude of hopelessness which surrounded our lives left me feeling stranded—swept in a rapids over which I had no control.

My association with Matt and his family had been an anchor in this sea of uncertainty. That tie was now severed. Perhaps it never existed as I had perceived it. I had come to grips with the breakup and had at last acknowledged to myself that it was better for each of us to break from each other.

Since there were fewer and fewer jobs available, I had long since given up hope of finding conventional employment. Most of the applicants had experience. I had none. News of openings was relayed by insiders to acquaintances who were hired before the vacancy was made known. It was known as *pull.* If you didn't have *pull,* you were out of luck. Employers were happy to be spared the expense of advertising and screening applicants.

I began to think about the kids I had graduated with. We had had good teachers, dedicated to making self-reliant citizens of us. Those of us who had stayed on to finish were hailed as the hope of the future. I wondered how many of them were doing anything worthwhile with their lives. Were they all drifting, as I was?

I had not seen Marjorie since graduation night now more than a year ago. One evening after supper, I dropped a nickel into the pay phone on the corner. There was a pay phone in the back hall at home for the convenience of the tenants, but I wanted to talk privately.

After a few rings, I heard the impersonal voice of the operator.

"The number you have just called has been disconnected."

"Disconnected?"

"Yes. Disconnected."

"Thank you."

Dejectedly, I hung the receiver on its hook and pushed open the folding door of the booth. I knew where Marjorie lived. I would walk over to her house tomorrow.

The "kid," as Uncle Frank referred to him, was dusting the cars on the lot as he did regularly. I had seen him there many times, tall and gangly with a thick crop of curly, strawberry blond hair. It shimmered under the lights.

"Evenin'," he called as I walked past.

"Good evening," I answered, slowing my pace.

"Out for a little stroll?"

"Yeah. Gotta do something."

He had stopped dusting.

I had stopped walking.

"You're Frank Roemer's niece?"

"Yes. How'd you know?"

"I've seen you around. Coming and going."

"I've seen you, too."

"Yeah?"

"Yeah."

"I'm gonna be through here in about fifteen minutes."

"I bet you're glad."

"O, it's not so bad. It's an easy job."

"It's almost nine o'clock. What time did you start?"

"I came in about three o'clock today. Schindler doesn't care what time I start. As long as it gets done a couple times a week. And after a rain."

"It hasn't rained for quite a few days," I commented.

"I think it's going to rain tonight."

"You do? Why?"

"I can smell it. Can't you?"

"Guess I haven't been paying attention," I said. "I guess I *can* smell it, now that you mention it."

"As soon as I'm through here, I'm going down the street to Werner's Drug Store and get myself an ice-cream cone."

"That sounds good," I said. "After a day's work, you deserve."

Turning to resume my walk toward the house, I called back over my shoulder, "Have a good time!"

"Want to come along?"

"What?" I stopped and turned.

"Come on along. I'll buy you an ice-cream cone."

I hesitated.

"Come on," he coaxed. "It's just a couple blocks. I'll walk back with you."

"Well~you're sure it's okay?"

"Would I ask you if it wasn't?"

"Okay." I waited while he went into the shack and did whatever it was he had to do before leaving. He joined me in a moment.

"What's your name?" he asked as we started toward the corner.

"Lindy."

"Lindy? That's kind of an unusual name."

"Well, it's Belinda, really. But my aunt's name is Belle, and I guess my mother thought there'd be too much confusion if they called me Belle, too. So they've always called me Lindy."

"Makes sense. I like the sound of *Lindy*. Reminds me of Lindbergh. *Lucky Lindy.*"

"What's your name?" I asked.

"Ray. Raymond, really. But you know how that is. Nobody calls me Raymond except my mother and then only when she's mad at me."

"She gets mad at you?"

"Yeah. Sometimes."

"Oh, my! Do you live around here?"

"Yeah. Not far. Around Nineteenth and Washington."

"Did you go to South Division High School?"

"Yeah. For a couple years. Then I dropped out."

"Dropped out?"

"Yeah. My old man got me fixed up in an apprenticeship. I was gonna be a tinsmith. But after six months, the tinsmith went bankrupt."

Our feet made a hollow sound on the wooden steps of the drug store. The screech of the screen door announced our arrival to the aproned couple behind the counter. A rotund gentleman wearing a straw hat was leaving carrying a half-dozen ice cream cones, their points projecting through holes cut into a cardboard box.

"Are you gonna eat all that?" Ray quipped to the stranger as he walked toward the door.

"Not all by myself," the gentleman answered cordially. He smiled as he shouldered the door open. "This is for the *porch brigade.*"

The door slammed noisily.

"What kind d'ya like?" Ray asked.

"I like 'em all," I answered. I was feeling much happier now than an hour ago.

"How 'bout chocolate?"

"Fine. I like chocolate."

"Two double chocolates," Ray said to the counterman.

"Wouldja like some jimmies with that?" the man asked.

"Okay. Jimmies." Ray responded.

The counterman smiled as he sprinkled a generous portion of the little chocolate "worms" over the tops and handed one to each of us. They were beautiful! Ambrosia! A feast for the gods.

Ray handed over a quarter, representing more than an hour's work, no doubt, and pocketed the nickel change.

The door screeched and slammed as we thumped down the steps to the sidewalk.

"My! Thank you!" I gushed. "They sure look good."

"They sure do, don't they?"

"I'm glad I happened by when I did. I didn't expect this tonight."

"I'm glad, too."

"How long have you been working for Schindler?"

"Just about all summer."

"Have you ever thought about going back to school?"

"Na-a-ah! The kids would laugh at me. I'm almost twenty years old, and I'd be a sophomore. Can you imagine what they'd do to me? They'd laugh me right out the door."

"Well, what're you going to do?" I asked.

"I dunno. Get a better job, maybe. What're *you* gonna do? Get married, I s'pose, and have a family. That's what girls usually do, 'specially pretty ones." He gave me an appraising look under the street light. "Yeah, you'll get married," he pronounced.

I didn't say anything, but I knew what I wanted. I wanted to be discovered. I wanted to sing like Helen Morgan and Kate Smith.

We sat on the steps of the front porch and lingered over the ice cream as long as we dared before it melted all over our fingers.

Chapter 13

True to Ray's prediction, we had had a good rain during the night. The wind had shifted to the north and brought down the first leaves of autumn. Damp and fragrant, they now covered the lawn and glistened in the cool sunshine.

I inhaled the crisp, clean air, then turned back into the house to get a sweater, the long, dark red one with the shawl collar. I looped the belt around my waist and mentally reviewed the route to Marjorie's house. I had visited her a few times while we were still high school chums.

Marjorie's mother, wearing a tan nondescript sweater over her cotton housedress, was out on the front porch sweeping leaves. A scarf was tied around her head. She was heavier now than I remembered.

"Good morning, Mrs. Van Allen," I greeted her.

A look of pleasure spread over her face as she recognized me.

"Lindy!" she exclaimed. "It's so good to see you. We have spoken of you so often, Marjorie and I. How have you been? Come in! Come in! It's time for a second cup of coffee. I'll call Marjorie. She lives upstairs now, you know."

No, I didn't know.

She hustled me inside, where yesterday's heat still lingered, talking all the while.

"How is everything with you, Lindy? Are you still singing? Come into the kitchen. I'll call Marjorie."

I seated myself at the oil-cloth covered kitchen table where a few crumbs were still visible. The breakfast dishes were drying in a wire basket on the drainboard of the sink.

Mrs. Van Allen stepped into the back hall and opened a door onto a stairway. Looking up into the stairwell, she called, "MARJORIE-E-E! . . . MARJORIE-E-E!" Then turning to me she said, "She'll be down in a minute," and busied herself with dumping the coffee grounds, rinsing the aluminum percolator, and preparing a fresh pot of coffee.

"You needn't go to a lot of trouble on my account, Mrs. Van Allen," I said, trying to put her at ease. "I tried to call you on the phone, but~"

"It's no trouble," she assured me. "I baked some bread yesterday, so I took some of the batter and made *Kaffee Kuchen*. You know," she confessed, "I hardly knew how to bake bread, but with the mister out of work, we had to get some help from the County, and you know~or maybe you don't~that when you're on the County, you bake your own bread or go without. So like everybody else, I had to learn. Now, if I say so myself, I can make pretty good bread~and *Kaffee Kuchen*, too. It's easy," she went on as she wiped the crumbs from the oil-cloth with a damp cloth. "You just add some eggs and a little sugar to the bread batter~ We get lots of raisins~ And cinnamon I had~

The upstairs door opened and Marjorie came through.

"Lindy! Lindy!"

We rushed into each other's arms, laughing, hugging, weeping.

Marjorie was pregnant! Grossly pregnant! I was speechless.

"Migod, Marjorie!" I exclaimed as I appraised her. "Why didn't you *tell* me? I'm completely bewildered. What's the meaning of all this?"

"Ja! ja!" her mother sighed and shook her head as she regarded her daughter's figure, whereupon Marjorie began to cry.

Marjorie blushed and contemplated her hands as they lay in her lap. She assumed, I guess, that I was still a virgin and she, of course, was a sinner. Poor Marjorie! It occurred to me that people who grew up in conventional households, with both parents, church affiliations, *normal* family ties, were terribly naive—and cruel, too.

I should have stayed home, I thought. *I've walked into a hornets' nest.*

Mrs. Van Allen came from the pantry with cups and saucers. She set a pressed-glass bowl of spoons on the table beside a matching sugur bowl and cream pitcher. They were purple with traces of gold trim still visible. A plate of *kuchen* squares appeared next. Then, in my honor, I presume, she brought linen napkins in silver rings. We didn't use them. It would have made more ironing.

Marjorie, leaving the table for a moment, went into her mother's bedroom and came back with an embroidered handkerchief with a crocheted edge. Mrs. Van Allen poured the coffee. It was hot and strong. We all relaxed a little.

"Well," Marjorie began, as if she owed me some explanation, "I'm married—now. But I wasn't married when I got this way."

"You're not the first," I tried to assure her.

"Oh, I know. That's what everybody says, but—" She nodded toward her mother who was, at that moment, seating herself heavily at the table.

The inference was immediately clear. Mamma was not going to let her daughter forget her *sin.*

"Who's the lucky young man?" I finally had the courage to ask.

"He's Casey—Casey Orlikowski. Do you remember him? He went to South Division, too."

"*Casey!*" Mrs. Van Allen sneered. "*Casimir* you mean. *Casey!*" she repeated derisively. She looked to me for support.

Insights were beginning to form. Marjorie Van Allen, Dutch Protestant, married to Casimir Orlikowski, Polish Catholic.

"The name is familiar. Wasn't he on the track team? He must

have left school—graduated probably—while I was still a freshman. Wasn't he part of an older group?"

"Yes," Marjorie agreed, "he's twenty-three. He's selling household products door-to-door. And we're getting some help from the County, too."

"Have some coffeecake," Mrs. Van Allen urged.

"Thank you. How's he doing?"

"Better than I would have thought."

"The coffeecake is very good, Mrs. Van Allen."

"Thank you, Lindy." She took a soggy handkerchief from her apron pocket, wiped her eyes and blew her nose.

"When is your baby due?"

"October. About six weeks."

"Are you excited about it?"

"Yeah. Getting excited. Casey's family had a shower for me. D'you wanna see what I got?" She was smiling happily. "C'mon upstairs."

"Okay." I turned to Mrs. Van Allen as I got up from my chair. "Are you coming, too?"

"No," she sighed. "I seen it all. You two go ahead."

"Will you excuse us, then?" I asked.

She shook her head and waved us out of the room.

"Thank you for the cake and coffee," I said as I shook her hand. "I'll be leaving, soon. The cake was very good. I'll have to remember how you do it."

"Goodbye, Lindy. Come again soon." There were tears in her eyes. Clearly, this was not what she had in mind for Marjorie.

I observed Marjorie's swollen ankles as she preceded me up the narrow stairs. At the top, she opened the door and we entered a small, neat kitchen. An embroidered tablecloth covered the white, enameled table. Cottage curtains graced a pair of windows which overlooked the back yard. Little plaques and pot holders decorated the pale yellow walls.

"This is charming!" I exclaimed to Marjorie.

"It's a little small, but it will do until we can get out of here."

I made no comment.

"C'mon," she said enthusiastically, "See the rest of it. There are only three rooms and a tiny bath."

She ushered me into a small living room in which were a sofa, obviously not new, a small rocker, and a lamp. A braided oval rug covered the floor. The corner of a hand-crocheted doily was displayed beneath the table radio as it rested on an end table against the wall.

She chattered happily as she explained to me that all of this had been attic space; and how her father and Casey, with some help from Casey's older brother, who was pretty clever with tools, had somehow pulled the materials together, most of it used, some of it donated, and had built this little flat.

She called my attention to the clever use of space under the eaves for closets and storage, and the bright corner of their bedroom beneath the gable which was occupied by a freshly enameled crib. Obviously coaxed out of its well-earned retirement in the corner of somebody's attic, it stood ready now—its teddy bear decals in place at head and foot, its clean white sheets and hand-made quilt of sunbonnetted figures—awaiting its new occupant.

The flat was a doll house. The very sparsity of its furnishings bespoke the *newlywed* status of its occupants.

"Just look at this!" she exclaimed at one point as I was contemplating—absorbing—this staggering glut of impressions.

"What?" .

She took my hand and placed it on her bulging abdomen. I felt the rearing baby as it rolled over and changed position inside her. I was aghast! Imagine being occupied by another human being!

My face must have revealed my shock, for she said reassuringly, "O, it's not so bad. Although sometimes I feel as though I'm black and blue inside. They tell me they quiet down as they get bigger and there's not enough room. That's when they want to get out."

I felt completely naive before this knowledgeable woman. She opened the chest beside the crib to reveal all the little clothes and accessories she had accumulated for this unknown person. Tiny sweaters and bonnets, booties, shirts and diapers. She interspersed this display with commentary which told the source of every item, which were new and which were used.

"What are these?" I asked, noting some straight flannel strips, each about three inches wide.

"Those? Bellybands," she informed me, matter-of-factly.

"Bellybands? What are they for?"

"Lindy! Are you teasing me? You're not really that dumb, are you?"

"'Fraid so," I admitted. "Please tell me, what are bellybands for?"
Marjorie laughed at me.

"What's so funny?" I asked.

"You look so serious."

"Marjorie, I'm bewildered by all this. It's just too much at once. I can't take it all in."

"I should be able to understand that. Until I found myself in this fix, I didn't have anything but vague notions. Then my mother told our insurance man I was pregnant, and he gave her some books for me. Here," she said, opening a dresser drawer, "these are some of the books I've been reading. See?"

She opened one of them to a well-thumbed page and pointed to an illustration. "See? This is what you do with a bellyband. The text explains what it's supposed to do."

The line drawing pictured the mid-section of an infant having its bellyband snugly pinned in place. The text instructed the new mother to keep a clean band on the infant to protect the navel until the umbilical cord dropped off.

"Casey's sister told me these instructions were written for mothers who deliver their babies at home. She said if I have the baby in a hospital, I might not need them at all because they keep you for ten days, and by that time, the cord has usually come off."

"Hmp!" I said. "Are you going to a hospital?"

"I'm eligible to go to County. I don't know," she said uncertainly. "My mother had us kids at home. I don't like being separated from the baby—you know—having it in the nursery. I want it with me."

She sighed. She was already aching with love for that little one. Even now, she could not bear the thought of being separated from it for even one moment.

"Still, everyone seems to think it's safer for both of us if I go to the hospital. What would you do, Lindy?"

What would I do? The situation was unimaginable to me. "Gee! Marjorie. I don't know." I wrinkled my brow and sighed, too. "I just don't know."

As I browsed through the pages, the illustrations filled me with wonder. While information of this kind had not been withheld from me, it had never had such impact before. Perhaps because it was personal—perhaps because it was Marjorie.

"Marjorie, you've become so—so—I don't know," I said despairingly. "So *grown-up!*"

"I hope you don't feel too alienated," she said as I was leaving. "I hope you'll come again."

"I'll keep in touch," I promised, hugging her.

The door closed behind me. I walked forward with a new view, conscious of having entered a new phase of my life.

Chapter 14

For a long time after I went to bed that night, I lay awake thinking about Marjorie. I imagined her in the old iron bed with Casey right now. Were they making love? *Could* they, with Marjorie's bulging belly intruding between them? Was the intrusion symbolic? Would the child always come between them?

Was she happy? Did she change her religion? Did *he?* Why was it important~important enough to affect Mrs. Van Allen as it had? How had they had dealt with it?

I visualized the little flat they lived in. So neat. Everything in its place. I began to conjure visions of what I would do with it if it were mine.

As I tossed on the lumpy old daybed, I began to ponder my situation. I had no private space. For the first time, I saw myself as deprived. I began to envy Marjorie. I, too, needed a place of my own.

At last, I drifted off to sleep while dreaming of myself arranging a fluffy valance on a rod over Marjorie's bedroom window.

As Marjorie's expected delivery date drew near, I dropped a nickel in the pay phone in the hall one afternoon and asked to speak to the Chief Operator. I gave her the Van Allens' old phone number and address and asked for a neighbor's number.

"'Allo!" a woman's voice answered in response to my call. Even in one word, I detected an accent.

"Hello!" I answered. "Please excuse this intrusion. I'm trying to contact Marjorie Orlikowski--Marjorie Van Allen. I believe she lives next door to your address."

"Yes, she does. I'll call her."

The woman was already on her way. I had prepared a lengthy explanation which apparently wasn't needed. The minutes seemed endless as I stood at the phone in the back hall, first on one foot, then the other, the receiver to my ear.

"Hello?" I heard at last. It was Mrs. Van Allen. "Hello? Who is this?"

"This is Lindy, Mrs. Van Allen."

"Who?"

"Lindy Albright. Marjorie's friend. Remember?"

"O-o-oh! Lindy!" A moment's reflection, then "How are you Lindy?"

"O, *I'm* fine. I'm calling to find out how Marjorie is."

"Marjorie's in the hospital. He took her this morning."

"This morning?"

"Yes. She went into labor during the night. We haven't heard anything yet. I thought when you called--"

"O, I'm sorry. I'll get off the line so he can get through to you. Where is she?"

"At County Hospital."

"I'll ride out there tomorrow," I promised.

So saying, I put on my coat, took my purse and headed for the dry goods store down the street. I selected a soft, white, fringed shawl, which Lydia tenderly folded into a tissue lined box. We had been buying stockings and garter belts from Lydia for a long time.

"For one of your friends?" she inquired, her black-brown eyes scrutinizing me. Lydia was very pretty, I thought. Her creamy complexion enhanced her tiny rosebud mouth, and her hair, black and shiny, was piled high on her head and caught up in a bun.

Why she was still a maiden lady was a puzzle to all of us.

"Yes, a high school chum."

"What did she have?"

"I don't know yet. I'm going to visit her tomorrow. I just talked to her mother on the phone. She still didn't know."

"Are you excited about it?"

"Yeah, I guess I am. A brand new human being!"

She looked thoughtfully at me. "Another generation!" she observed. "I suppose you'll be next."

The thought jolted me. "Not yet!" I exclaimed. Maybe later, but I knew what I wanted first. I wanted to sing and get paid for it. Not a piddly ten-dollar-bill after a night's work, or a prize on talent night—provided there wasn't a magician or a trained-dog act on the show. Why, Margaret Whiting was getting seventy-five dollars a side as a singer with orchestras making records!

"That'll be two dollars," Lydia said.

❀   ❀   ❀

Marjorie was in a state of elation when I found her sitting up in her hospital bed. Her husband held her hand as he sat beside her, smiling. He wore a suit and tie in keeping with his job as a salesman.

"He's beautiful!" she gushed as we embraced. "O, Lindy! I held him! I held him! You'll have to go to the nursery and see him. Casey will go with you. He's only seen him once."

Casey and I regarded each other cautiously.

"Omigosh! You two don't know each other, do you? I'm sorry. Lindy, this is my husband, Casey. Casey, this is my old friend, Lindy."

"How d'ye do?" we stammered as we timidly shook hands across the bed.

A spray of freckles across his nose accented the merriment in his hazel eyes. He looked at his watch. "It's just about time," he said. "They'll be showing the babies now."

We left Marjorie happily removing ribbon and tissue from the gift I brought and walked toward the nursery where Casey displayed a little card against the glass. I studied all the tiny ones, each in its little crib, each with its own distinctive features.

"There he is!" Casey said, pointing to a red-faced, robust infant with a shock of black hair.

"How do you know?" I asked. "You've only seen him once."

"I *know*," he answered confidently. "He looks just like my old man."

*　　*　　*

November brought the long awaited election which swept Roosevelt into the presidency. The long wait until inauguration proved an embarrassment to the Hoover administration which did everything it could to save face in defeat. "Immediate and complete reorganization of the banking system," and "reduction in government salaries," were among the proposals offered.

The outgoing administration would be credited with the adoption of the Twentieth Amendment which changed inauguration date from March 4, the anniversary date of the Constitution, to January 20. Also, the Twenty-first Amendment, repealing prohibition, was passed by the Senate and sent to the States for ratification before Hoover left office.

As worried depositors withdrew their funds from banks, the money supply was drying up. The City of Milwaukee, with authorization of the Clearing House Association, printed thirty-two million dollars worth of scrip, backed by delinquent real estate taxes, to maintain essential services, such as schools, police and fire departments.

At considerable risk to himself, Harve became our bank. The National Trust Company closed before Uncle Frank and Aunt Belle could cash their paycheck. Harve cashed their checks as well as Mother's since the school's bank had also closed.

Stan, from Apartment 5, and the couple who now lived in Apartment 4 paid their rent in checks of small denominations which they had received from their employers. They were made

"Payable to Bearer" so they could circulate like cash and not reach the bank all at once.

On March 1, six states declared a bank holiday to prevent further panic withdrawals. On inauguration day, three days later, Governor Lehman declared a state bank holiday in the State of New York. Governor Horner, following his lead, closed all the banks in Illinois, while the new president told us in his inaugural address that "[t]he only thing we have to fear is fear itself."

There followed a spate of legislation that had never been witnessed before and probably never would be again. It began the day after the inauguration in March, a Sunday, when the new president called a special session of Congress to approve a national week-long bank holiday. One week later, in a "fireside chat," the first of many for which he would become known, he took the nation into his confidence concerning his plans for the future.

The banks began reopening the following day and one month later, almost all of them were doing business as usual.

As the amendment to repeal prohibition continued its march from state to state seeking ratification, Harve and his associate, Dunbar, whom I had never met, began to cast about for a site for their proposed supper club. Both men had done well financially as bootleggers and were eager now to invest their cache in a solid, lawful enterprise.

Alas, no Hollywood scouts had appeared at any of my Talent Night performances. I had not been whisked away to Hollywood on a wave of glitz and glamour. I was forced to come to grips with the reality that it wasn't going to happen unless I made it happen.

Begging a sheet of Aunt Belle's grey stationery with the silver deckle edge and a matching envelope, I had written a letter to KSEN, one of the three local radio stations, requesting an audition. I had given a resume of my experience, citing the names of various theaters and churches where I had performed. Sure that they received twenty such requests each day, I really did not expect a favorable response. So it was with some misgiving that, one summer day, I opened a letter addressed to me with the KSEN logo on the envelope.

"Well, what do they say?" Aunt Belle asked as she rearranged Uncle Frank's shirt on the ironing board.

"They want me to come for an audition."

"Really?! When?"

"At two o'clock Wednesday." I was elated.

"What are you going to sing?"

"Gee, I don't know yet. Maybe *'Paper Moon'* for one. They say I should prepare three."

"How 'bout *'Temptation'*?" Aunt Belle asked. "I heard you do that one at the Granada Theater. You did it well."

"What do you think of *'Who's Afraid of the Big Bad Wolf?'*"

"That sounds good. Each one is a different style."

"I think I'll work on those three. Sure wish I had a piano. And somebody to play it. It's kind of hard to practice without an accompanist."

Aunt Belle's iron skated smoothly across the board. "Why don't you ask Harve if you can practice at his friend's place," she suggested. She draped the shirt on the back of a chair.

"His friend? What friend?"

"You know. The one he's going into business with. What's-his-name."

"Dunbar?"

"Yeah. Dunbar."

"At the *speakeasy?*"

"Why not? There's probably no one around during the day."

I chuckled naughtily as I considered it. "I don't know. I'll have to think about it."

"Sure, think about it," Aunt Belle urged. "It's just a matter of time now before it's a perfectly legal enterprise anyway. Several states have already ratified."

"I know. I read that they expect that amendment to zip through before the end of the year. Every three-point-two saloon in town is getting a paint job."

"Not *saloon*, Lindy! Roosevelt says they're now *' taverns.'* I guess that's supposed to make them more respectable! More *folksy!"*

We laughed together as she carried on, bending to the basket of dampened laundry, occasionally wiping the perspiration from her face. Her cotton housedress stuck to her damp back as she stretched a starched apron across the ironing board.

"People who go to *saloons* get drunk," she declared, "but people who go to *taverns* are just having a well-deserved good time."

"Sit down and have a cold drink," I told her. "It must be the heat. You're getting silly! I'll finish the ironing."

୬୨

Chapter 15

While talking to Mother on the phone that week, I asked her to make a special effort to remember to invite Harve to have dinner with us Thursday night. She must have been curious, but she complied without comment. At dinner, I announced my appointment to have an audition at KSEN the following week.

"Good for you!" Harve was enthusiastic.

"Isn't it wonderful?" Aunt Belle beamed. "It might be just the opportunity she's been waiting for."

"Don't get your hopes up," Mother cautioned. "Remember you're just one in a million."

"She's going to do just fine," Uncle Frank said confidently. "She's as good as any of 'em."

"There's just one hitch," I announced.

"What's that?" Harve asked.

"I'd like to rehearse with a piano. Does your friend have a piano at his place?"

"Yeah, there's a piano there. They have an orchestra for dancing on weekends."

"Do you suppose he'd let me use it during the day when there aren't any customers around?"

"Don't see why not. Do you want me to talk to him about it?"

"Would you please? I would surely appreciate it."

The next day, Harve called me.

"Lindy?"

"Yes?"

"Dunbar says you can come down any day after 10:00 a.m.. The place will be locked, but he'll let you in. You'll have to call him and let him know about what time you'll be there. He'll watch for you. Okay?"

"Okay. Thanks. And Harve?"

"Yes?"

"What does Dunbar look like. I've never met him."

"That's right. You never have. Well,—" He was silent a moment. "Tell you what. I'll come and pick you up and take you over there myself and introduce you."

"Oh, that would be wonderful! You're sure it's not too much trouble? I don't know where the place is—and I feel a little—*funny*—about going into a place like that alone."

"Yeah. You should have somebody with you. I'll stay with you while you rehearse if you want me to."

"Will you have time?"

"I'll *make* time," he said, laughing.

"Well,—thank you," I sputtered, trying to believe what I was hearing. "How about tomorrow morning. I'd like to get in as much practice as I can."

"Okay. Tomorrow at ten. See you then."

"You know," I commented to Aunt Belle as I hung the receiver, "there may be some hope for him after all."

"Some *hope?*"

"I'm afraid I'm beginning to like him."

❀ ❀ ❀

True to his word, Harve appeared at the door the next morning just before ten o'clock. I grabbed my purse and my music from the dining-room table and we were on our way.

"I'm glad you spoke up yesterday," Harve remarked as we got

under way. "Dunbar's place is not in a very good neighborhood for a young lady to be running around alone. What you need is a boyfriend to take you around."

"What I need is a car of my own," I countered.

"A *car of your own!*" he exclaimed. "Independent little so-and-so, aren't ya? You can't even drive!"

"I could learn—same as you." I could feel another argument emerging. I really didn't want it to happen. He was going out of his way to do me a big favor.

"Well, maybe if you get this big job at KSEN, you might be able to get your own car," he said, a note of sarcasm in his voice. "Your Uncle Frank ought to be able to pick up a pretty good deal for you there on Schindler's lot."

"That would be nice," I said. *What a pretty dream,* I thought. "Then maybe I could do *you* a favor some time."

"Do *me* a favor, eh?" The concept was shockingly novel to him.

"Well, why not? You're a pretty decent guy. You're doing a favor for me."

"You think I'm a pretty decent guy, do you?"

"Yeah, you're okay."

"Just okay?"

"Yeah."

He reflected on that for a moment. I thought he repressed a smile.

"What happened to Matt?" he asked. "I haven't seen him around lately."

I was surprised that he should ask me so bluntly about something that was none of his business. Might this indicate a fatherly interest in *me?* I gave him the benefit of the doubt.

"Matt thought it would be better for both of us if we dated others—at least for awhile."

"He's still going to school, isn't he?"

"Yes."

"Maybe he's right. Maybe he's a little more grown-up—a little more *mature*, as they say nowadays—than you."

He was making me angry again—making assumptions without bothering to find out what my view was.

"It so happens," I said haughtily, "that I'm in total agreement with Matt."

As I stared through the windshield, I caught a glimpse of Harve looking at me. He stroked his nose as if he had taken a blow.

I would be careful about extending an olive branch in the future.

We drove into a brick-paved alley and parked in a space behind a cement-block building that looked like a warehouse. I was already out of the car when he came around to open the door for me.

"Follow me," he instructed as he walked toward a heavy, un-painted door. Selecting a key from his key ring, he pulled the door open onto a long hall. He pushed a light button on the wall as he stepped inside. A single bare bulb hung from the ceiling. I followed. The door fell shut behind me.

Ye gods! What a crummy place! I thought.

Choosing another key, he opened the door onto a darkened area where the combined redolence of booze and nicotine made me squint and wrinkle my nose.

"Anybody here?" he called.

A square of daylight appeared as a portion of the back wall swung inward illuminating a barroom.

"Yo! Right here," came a brassy baritone.

I followed Harve behind the bar and into the brightly lighted office. Inside was a huge rolltop desk in an astonishingly ordered state. A few chairs stood around a card table while a safe occupied the far corner of the room.

Harve extended his hand to a black-haired man, taller and, surprisingly, younger than himself. I had assumed that Harve's business associates would be near his own age.

After the two men greeted each other, their attention turned to me and my reason for being there.

"This is Lindy Albright," Harve introduced me. "Lindy, this is

Dunbar."

"How do you do, Mr. Dunbar."

"*Mister* Dunbar?" He laughed as he shook my hand. "Miss Albright. Mind if I call you 'Lindy'?" His smile showed good, even teeth. He was rather good looking.

"That's okay, I guess."

"We came to use the piano for a little while, if that's all right with you," Harve explained.

"Sure, it's okay." Like the lens of a camera, his eyes photographed me: the locket at my throat, the buttons of my blouse, the buckle at my waist. "You gonna hang around?"

"Yeah, I'll stay with 'er. It's only for a couple days. She'll have her audition on Wednesday."

"Well, good luck, Lindy. Come this way. I'll show you where the piano is."

When we turned back into the barroom, all the lights were on. A young man worked with a polishing cloth behind the bar. A room I had not seen on entering was now fully illuminated. Chairs were turned upside-down onto tabletops. A woman was using a vacuum cleaner. In the center was a square of hardwood floor for dancing. My heels were noisy as we walked across it. On a raised dais just beyond its perimeter, the piano could be seen.

"A baby grand!" I exclaimed. "Nice." I struck a few treble keys, then a few bass. I opened *Paper Moon* onto the music rack, found my pitch and hummed. "I'm going to do a few warmup exercises which aren't very interesting."

"Fire away!" Dunbar said.

They turned back toward the office.

"Thanks, Mr. Dunbar."

"*Dun*bar!" he corrected.

After a few *lalalas,* I swung into it, getting the feel. I caught a glimpse of the cleaning lady as I sang. She was watching, smiling, polishing the same table over and over. I saw her exchange approving glances with the young man behind the bar.

The Big Bad Wolf was indeed dead without any accompaniment. I tried to plunk it out with one finger, then gave it up and concentrated on enunciation and breath control. I would have to hope for the best.

"Want a little help with that?" I heard beside me.

I turned to find the dark-haired fellow who'd been polishing glasses. I was doubtful. A bartender?

He slid onto the piano bench, examined the music, tickled a few keys, then confidently struck the introductory chords. As he convinced me that he could really play, I got into the fun spirit of the tune. It came off pretty well. By the time he'd rippled through the finale, we were laughing.

"That was fun. You sing okay!"

"Thank you!"

"Are you gonna sing here?" he asked.

"No," I explained. "I'm going to have an audition at KSEN. I'm just rehearsing here because I don't have a piano at home."

"I see. Want to try the other one while you're here?" he asked, paging through my music.

"Yes," I said. "I want to get as much practice as I can between now and Wednesday."

"What's your name?" he asked. "I'd like to know it in case I read about you in the newspapers—you know—after you get famous."

I smiled at such a projection. "Well, for the record, my name is Lindy Albright, but don't look for it in lights yet. You're not likely to find it very soon—if *ever*."

"The *Lindy* is good," he said seriously, "but I don't know about the Albright. Too *German*. Too—*provincial*. Have you ever considered taking a stage name?"

"No, I never have. Do you think I should?"

"Yeah," he breathed. "Ma-a-n! You're *good!*"

No member of my own family had ever expressed this much confidence in me. Not even Matt.

"How'd you like to take a break? Have a drink?"

"I don't drink."

"Soft drink?"

"Okay. What do you have?"

"All kinds," he called on his way to the bar. "Cherry, cream, root beer~"

"I'd like orange if you have some."

"One orange~coming up."

I stepped off the dais and sat at one of the tables. The cleaning lady, on her way out of the room, fumbled at a bank of light switches darkening the room again except for a few spots over the dais. The young man joined me in a moment with the drinks. They were cold and refreshing.

"What's *your* name?" I asked as I took the drink from his hand.

"Bret."

I looked suspiciously at him. "Is that a stage name?"

"Yeah," he admitted. "My mother named me *Gilbert*. But I don't like it. People either call you *Gilly* or *Bert* and I didn't like either one. So I took the part of my name that was least offensive to me, rearranged the letters and came up with *Bret*.

"Okay," I laughed. "Bret it is."

The orange drink felt good to my parched throat. "They smoke a lot in here, don't they?" I said, grimacing.

"Yeah, they sure do. The place is blue sometimes."

"I guess I'd better get busy," I said as I finished my drink. "Harve doesn't want to spend the whole day here, I'm sure."

"Okay," Bret agreed. "Let's have at it. What's the next one?"

"*Temptation.*"

"This should be good."

Carefully, meticulously, he worked through the accompaniment, familiarizing himself with every trill, every nuance.

"Okay," he said. "I think I'm ready for you."

I did a few *mi-mi-mis*. Then, following his throbbing intro, I opened on a low throaty note. Uncertain at first, we gradually gained confidence in each other~then leaned together into the pulsating rhythm of the lament. As the melody reached its climax, all the longing that I had kept bottled up for so long poured forth. I felt myself gliding on the ice with Matt. I felt again the joy of fulfillment in our intimate moments together. I felt my despair—my *utter* despair—at losing him.

We glided to a close. It wasn't until after the last note had trembled into silence that I became aware of three figures silhouetted in a frame of bright sunlight behind the bar where the office door had swung open. Harve, Dunbar and the cleaning lady. They were applauding!

Bret left the piano bench and embraced me!

"You're gonna make it!" he told me. "You're gonna make it—big!"

Chapter 16

Will Rogers and Jimmy Durante had no trouble finding material with which to lampoon the new administration. Month after month, as new government agencies were announced, the Civilian Conservation Corps (CCC), the Agricultural Adjustment Act (AAA), FERA, TVA, NRA, etcetera, it was feared by the radio comedians that another alphabet would have to be devised to accommodate the White House. Jokes were rampant as the mood of the country changed from one of despair to one of hope.

By mid-year, 1933, more than a million-and-a-half of the twenty-four million persons displaced by the depression had found employment.

Harve and Dunbar, after casting about for a site, had found acreage north and west of the city on a proposed east-west highway which promised to become a leading thoroughfare from the city to the state capitol. Here they hoped to build a plush-and-chrome supper club featuring the top entertainers in the field.

Bret had volunteered to go with me to the audition at KSEN as my accompanist. We had practiced together several times and knew each other's moves, so it seemed like a reasonable thing to do. KSEN had no objection and it was reassuring to have him with me. The audition went well.

"Thanks, Bret," I said as we left the studio. "If anything good comes of this, it will be because of your help and support."

"I got the feeling while we were in there that they were impressed," he said. "I think they'll come through with something for you. Why don't we go someplace and have something? A treat? What do you like? How about an ice-cream soda?"

"Okay," I answered. "Now that it's over, I'm in a mood to celebrate."

"There's a nice ice-cream parlor just a couple blocks from here."

"You know," I commented later as we sipped our sodas, "you play very well. Why are you tending bar? Why aren't you playing with a band?"

"I *do* play with a band—the band that plays at Dunbar's place on weekends."

"Well, why were you behind the bar polishing glasses when I first saw you?"

"Because Harve asked me to be around when you came. He thought it would be better for you to have somebody around who could play the piano."

"*Harve?*"

"Yeah. Why does that surprise you?"

"Well, you may already know, Harve is my mother's boyfriend, and Harve and I have clashed a few times. To think he would ask you to help me—well—I'm surprised—and a little *touched* by it."

Later, as he parked in front of the house, he said, "Are you one of them, too?"

"One of what?"

"Well, you speak of Harve as your mother's boyfriend. Are your parents divorced?"

A million lies chased each other around my head. How was I going to answer him? Always we had tried to give the impression that my father was dead without actually saying so. Mother would speak of *The War* and its tremendous cost in terms of personal sacrifice. She was never specific, but somehow left the impression that her husband had died in the war. She had kept her maiden name, always signing simply *Elizabeth Albright*, and although she never wore a wedding ring, she was usually addressed as *Mrs.*

I was silent so long that Bret finally said, "I'm sorry. I had no right to ask."

My relief at being excused must have shown in my face.

Bret smiled and changed the subject. "I'd like to call you to find out what comes of the audition. May I do that?"

"Why, of course, although you'll probably be seeing Harve around. He'll know."

"I don't always see Harve. We aren't always there at the same time. Why don't you give me your number?"

✹　　✹　　✹

A couple of weeks went by while I examined the mail every day. At last it came—a fifteen-minute slot, Monday through Friday, 5:45 p.m. leading into the six o'clock news, with a staff pianist playing accompaniment. It was a significant slot for a beginner, and my first real job. I would be on the payroll as soon as I signed a contract.

Of course, the new job was the subject of dinner-table conversation the next Thursday evening when we were all together.

"A contract, eh?" Harve said thoughtfully. "You really ought to have an agent—someone to protect your interests and see that you're getting a fair deal."

"I'm really not in a position to question their offer," I said. "I'm glad to have a job." *Why did he always have to be so defensive? Didn't he trust anybody?*

"It wouldn't hurt to have a lawyer take a look at that contract," Uncle Frank supported him. "Just to be on the safe side. Besides, you're still a minor."

"Being a minor is a nuisance," I complained. "Do you know a lawyer, Harve?"

"Yeah, I've had occasion to consult one from time to time. Got his name from Dunbar. I've got his card right here."

We were all silent as he reached for his wallet, pretending not to remember his stint in a Cleveland jail.

"Here it is. *Jack Rottman.*" He handed the card to me. "Copy the information. I'd like to keep the card."

"Okay," I said, taking the card reluctantly. *Rottman?* The name did not inspire confidence. "Is he any good?"

"He's handled our affairs all right," Harve assured me.

"Well, I'll give him a call."

❋ ❋ ❋

The bare hardwood floor creaked as I stepped into the waiting room of Mr. Rottman's office above a hardware store on the east end of National Avenue. On my right as I entered, a large, middle-aged woman working at an Underwood typewriter finished typing a paragraph before looking up to acknowledge my presence. Cape-like sleeves of black chiffon with big red roses fell over her fleshy arms. The dark down on her upper lip formed a noticeable mustache. She wore rhinestone earrings.

"May I help you?" she said at last. I recognized her deep voice as that of the person I had spoken to on the phone when making the appointment. I thought I had been speaking to Mr. Rottman himself.

"I'm Miss Albright," I announced. "I phoned for an appointment."

"O, yes." She tilted her head to accommodate her bifocals as she looked through her appointment book. "Please be seated. Mr. Rottman has a client with him now."

She, too, looked me over from head to foot, as Dunbar had, but not approvingly.

Voices could be heard from inside the office. I selected a *National Geographic* from an oak library table in the middle of the room and seated myself in a straight chair as far from the brass cuspidor as I could get.

After a few moments, the office door opened and two elderly men emerged almost obscured by a cloud of cigar smoke.

"What's this?" the stout gentleman carrying his hat asked the other, whom I presumed to be Mr. Rottman. "A young lady? She has business with you?" he questioned the lawyer.

"She has an appointment. Yes," he answered.

"Hmph!" The cigar smoker tugged at the vest which spanned his protruding middle. "Women! Think they can do everything nowadays," he mumbled. He arranged his hat on his bald head as he shuffled toward the door. "A young woman like that should have her father with 'er."

Mr. Rottman winked at me and beckoned me into his office as the outer door closed. The secretary peered at us over her glasses and I wondered if she might be Mr. Rottman's wife. She need not have worried, I mused. I had no designs on her husband—or boss—whatever their relationship might be.

With a gesture, he indicated a chair as he moved behind the desk. He was a man of average height with white hair and deep lines in his long, slender face. He wore a dark suit. After gathering the documents on the desk into a folder, he extended his hand in greeting.

"How do you do, Miss—"

"Albright," I reminded him as I shook his hand. "Lindy Albright."

"What brings you here, Miss Albright?"

"I was referred to you by Harve—" It occurred to me that I didn't know his last name. "I'm sorry, I don't know his last name," I admitted, "but he's an associate of Mr. Dunbar."

"O, yes," Mr. Rottman said, recognizing the name and looking askance at me. "And what is the nature of your problem, Miss Albright?"

"Well," I took the envelope from my purse, "my family thought it would be a good idea to have this contract examined by an attorney before I sign it. I, personally, don't have any qualms about it, but I'd appreciate your opinion."

Taking the paper from my hand, he leaned back in his black leather-upholstered chair and adjusted his wire-rimmed glasses. After a few moments, he sat upright at his desk and, removing his glasses, asked, "How old are you?"

"Nineteen."

"Still a minor. Your parents will have to co-sign."

"That will delay the signing," I began to explain. "I don't live with my mother. I see her only about once a week."

"Who do you live with?"

"My aunt and uncle. My mother's sister and her husband."

"How long have you lived with them?"

"O, two—two-and-a-half years."

"Do your aunt and uncle have legal guardianship of you?"

"I don't think so."

"Have there ever been any legal papers drawn up—any court proceeding in Children's Court?"

"No."

"Where's your father?"

I felt my face grow hot. "I don't know." It was an honest answer.

"Who supports you?"

"I've been supporting myself ever since I graduated from high school."

"How do you support yourself?"

"I occasionally sing with a group that plays at wedding dances. Sometimes I sing at weddings and at theaters, too, when they have a talent night."

"You're a freelance singer?"

"Yes." I'd never thought of myself in that light before.

"And you earn enough to support yourself?"

"Yes."

"You pay your aunt a little room and board, do you?"

"Yes."

"Where's your mother?"

I told him of mother's job at the dormitory of the school.

"Does she contribute to your support?"

"She brings me gifts. Clothes, once in a while."

"But you pay for your own room and board and you've been separated from your mother for over two years."

"Yes." This was a cold, but accurate, analysis of my situation.

"And you don't know where your father is. How long since you've seen your father?"

"I've never seen him."

"It looks to me like you're emancipated," he said.

"Emancipated? I'm afraid I don't understand."

"It means you're an emancipated minor--that you can sign your own papers and do as you please. You've attained majority status. You don't live under your parents' roof. You're earning your own living. You can make your own decisions."

I was stunned for a moment. It was what I'd been wanting, but-- Suddenly I was standing on my own feet! My spine stiffened.

I watched him examine the document again. "Is this your first job?"

"Yes."

"You've read the contract?"

"Yes."

"You understand, then, that this is a thirteen-week contract. You're to be paid ten dollars for each performance--that's fifty dollars a week!--until such time as the show picks up a sponsor. You understand that?"

"Yes."

"You understand, too, that if no sponsor is forthcoming, your contract expires at the end of thirteen weeks?"

"Yes, I understand."

"Now," he went on, "if a sponsor should materialize, the contract is subject to re-negotiation."

"I see."

"At a higher figure, I presume. Apparently you don't have an agent--else you wouldn't be *here*."

"That's right. I wouldn't have any idea how to go about getting a reliable agent," I admitted.

"Hmm! I don't know much about that either," he conceded. "I haven't had the good fortune to deal with theatrical people." He shifted his position and looked at me *deferentially*, I thought. Did he consider me a *celebrity*? "But I'll look into it for you," he promised, "—with your permission, of course."

With my permission? Never in my life had anyone ever asked my permission! For anything!

Grasping the moment, I thought of Dunbar. Might he have some connection with such a person? He had hired the orchestra Bret played in.

"Well,—" I put him off, "I'll give your suggestion some thought. I may be in touch with you about it later. I'm going to take one thing at a time."

"You're a very lucky young lady, you know. There have been many weeks in recent years when I was lucky see fifty dollars—not that I didn't have it on the books, but I still don't know if I'll ever see some of it. And I struggled through seven years of college to get this far."

"*My!*" I responded, trying to express in one word my utmost respect for his effort.

"Have you spent any time at college, Miss Albright?"

"No."

"You're going to have the money to do it now," he counseled me. "I'd like to see you give it some thought."

"I'll do that, sir."

"This contract is okay. If KSEN—or anyone else—questions your signature, refer them to me."

"Thank you!"

As I rose and reached across the desk to shake his hand, he said, "Stop at the desk and see my secretary before you leave," thereby illustrating the balance of responsibility with freedom.

❧

Chapter 17

My footsteps rapped against the bare floor as I left the secretary's desk. I opened the door onto the brown-tan hall. Turning to close it behind me, I caught a glimpse of Mr. Rottman still standing at the threshold of his office watching me thoughtfully. The long stairway was interrupted by a landing. At last I reached the sidewalk and pensively made my way to the car stop. I intended to put off savoring my new status until after I had boarded the friendly old double 18, but the streetcar was so slow in coming and my head was so full that I could not wait. By the time it arrived, I had weighed almost all the implications so that very little was left to muse upon.

The future was opening like a magic book. The possibilities were endless. I, who had not yet seen one paycheck, saw myself with a place of my own—a real bedroom with a real bed, one that didn't have to be stripped and folded up every morning and made up again every night. I pictured myself owning *and driving* a car.

College? Well—maybe. Some of my basic needs would have to be satisfied first. I needed a home.

❀   ❀   ❀

The construction of the supper club had begun on Capitol Drive. Harve and Mother drove out there to watch its progress at every opportunity. On one occasion, they invited me to join them. Never having been a part of any such project and curious to know what was going on, I eagerly accepted their invitation.

I sat in the back seat of Harve's shiny new blue Ford two-door coach, Uncle Frank's first new-car sale. Uncle Frank had become top man on the used car lot and loved his work declaring he would never go back to the foundry.

Mother, while sitting up front with Harve, turned to him as we rode and muttered something I could not understand.

"Sure," Harve answered. "Go ahead and tell her. "Gotta tell somebody sooner or later."

Mother turned toward me.

"Lindy?"

"Yes?"

"I want you to be the first to know. Harve and I are going to be married."

"M-married?"

"Yes. We went for the license today."

"When? Where?" I asked, completely surprised.

"Next week Saturday. At the Courthouse."

"At the Courthouse?" I was relieved. I would not be asked to sing. I didn't think I could do it. "Do Aunt Belle and Uncle Frank know?"

"Not yet. We intend to tell them tonight at dinner."

"I'm happy for both of you," I said, putting an arm over the shoulder of each. "May I come?"

"Of course," Harve said, twinkling in a way I had not seen before. "It wouldn't be complete without you."

When we finally reached the building site, I was impressed by the trucks and the number of men at work. The excavation had been completed and footings were being poured. Drain tiles and cement blocks were visible on the premises while in the yet unpaved street, the city was installing sewer and water mains . Altogether, the project appeared to have generated much activity as well as curiosity in the neighborhood.

As we walked around and over the hills of excavated earth,

Harve pointed with pride to this feature and that as though visualizing it would make it materialize before our eyes.

"You know," he said to me as we stood peering down into the hole, "your mother has a share in this, too."

"Well," I said, "I hope it will be a profitable venture for both of you—*all* of you," I corrected myself remembering Dunbar was also a partner.

There was no lack of material for conversation that Thursday night. The big news, of course, was the upcoming wedding. Uncle Frank and Harve shook hands and slapped each other's shoulders while Mother and Aunt Belle hugged and laughed and cried.

Aunt Belle had prepared a platterful of golden pork chops which she served with apple sauce, boiled potatoes, and creamed cucumbers. Having spent a couple of hours outside at the building site, we had no trouble doing justice to Aunt Belle's delicious offerings.

Not wishing to detract from the impact of Mother's coming wedding, I held back my announcement until the end of the meal when I mentioned that I had been to see Harve's lawyer, Mr. Rottman.

"You went to see him, did you? I'm glad you did that. Did he examine the contract?"

"Yes, he did. He explained it all to me. He also counseled me in a couple of other areas."

"Counseled you?" Mother asked. "What kind of counsel? What did he advise?"

"He advised me to go to college now that I will have both the time and the money. He also told me that I am no longer a minor."

"How can that be?" Mother wanted to know. "You're not twenty-one yet."

"He said that because I've been self-supporting since before I graduated from high school, and I don't live under my parents' roof, and because I've been separated from my parents for more than two years, for those reasons I am what he called 'emancipated.'"

There was silence for a moment. Then Mother began to cry. "It sounds so cold and uncaring," she wailed, "as though I abandoned you. You know I didn't do that."

"Yes, I know," I said, taking her hand as she sat beside me at the table. "I just grew up." I didn't tell her that I had often *felt* abandoned. The facts were speaking for themselves, and for me, too. "It's really nothing to weep about. It was inevitable. It just means that I can sign my own contracts and make my own decisions."

"She's right," Harve agreed while placing his arm around Mother's shoulders. "She's a very mature young woman and you should be proud of her. If you'd have heard her sing *Temptation* over at the club, you'd *know* she's a woman now and not your little girl any more."

He glanced across the table at Uncle Frank. I saw the look that passed between them. Aunt Belle saw it, too. Her cup clattered noisily against the saucer. She rose and began clearing the dinner plates from the table.

"How about some chocolate cake?" she inquired. "I think it would be a nice way to celebrate Lindy's 'coming of age.' There's fresh coffee."

Chapter 18

"Lindy, will you please get that box down for me? The one on the closet shelf? I can't reach it."

We were together in Mother's dormitory room, packing her belongings to move into the flat which she and Harve would occupy. Each of us had changed since living apart. I think her real motive for inviting me was to become reacquainted before "forsaking all others." As we filled cartons with shoes and hand-bags, we reaffirmed our bond while establishing our separateness.

I rose from the edge of the narrow bed where I'd been sitting, and reached above her head. "Here you are. What's in it?"

"I'll have to look," she confessed.

"Hats!" we both exclaimed, giggling like two school girls.

Standing before the mirror, I tried on a deep green Empress Eugenie, the corner perched jauntily over one eye, one long green feather sweeping up and back assertively like a wing on the head of Mercury. It was quite a contrast to my almost-red hair.

"What do you think?" I chuckled.

"It looks swell! It really does," she laughed. Then suddenly serious, she said, "My God, Lindy! What a beautiful woman you are!"

Woman? My mother was acknowledging my adulthood?

"Thank you," I said awkwardly.

She fumbled for a handkerchief and wiped her nose. Her eyes were misty. I placed the hat back in the box.

"Would you like to have the hat?"

"No, Dear. They're kind of outdated now. They were popular a couple of years ago."

"I guess I should get rid of some of this rubbish," she said. "There's another box up there. Will you get it for me, please?"

I brought it down from the shelf and placed it on the bed. She lifted the lid as if fearing something alive would attack her.

"Pictures!" she exclaimed. "Old snapshots. A couple of studio photos, too, I think. There should be one of you--taken when you were a baby."

"Did I ever see it?"

"O, I think you did--when you were little. I haven't looked at them for years."

We each picked up a handful and shuffled through them.

"Here it is," she said, handing me a picture in a folder.

I scrutinized the strange child who looked at me from the photo, the round eyes, the plump cheeks, a bow tied into a large curl atop my head.

"Who did I look like?"

"Not like your father. Maybe you looked like somebody in his family--mother--grandmother-- I never met any of his family."

I thought of Matt, and how history had, indeed, repeated itself. We had both felt the pain of rejection. It was the same situation except that I had had the good luck (and luck it was,) not to become pregnant the very first time we made love. I may have had Matt's brother and their male camaraderie to thank that I did not become pregnant subsequently.

"You surely don't look like any of us--Belle or me--or Grandma."

"Do you have a picture of my father?"

"Only in a group."

"May I see it?"

She pawed through the contents of the box until I suspected she might be deliberately withholding it from me. At last she withdrew a post-card sized snapshot of several young men. "It was taken at a citizens' military training camp where he spent a couple of weeks every summer."

My father was the tallest of the lot, slim and handsome. I could easily understand how my mother fell in love with him.

"You may keep that if you like."

I studied it under the lamp. "I want very much to have it."

She gathered a few loose earrings from the dresser top and, as she opened her jewelry case to deposit them inside, she removed the chain with the black-onyx signet ring attached.

"I want you to have this, too," she said as she placed it in my palm and closed my fingers over it. "It belonged to your father. I owe it to Harve to put this old romance behind me."

It was only a *thing*, an *object*, yet it had a profound significance to me. I had asked her about it once when I was about five years old. She told me then that it came from someone she once loved who was now gone. As I grew older, I suspected the person she spoke of was my father.

As I placed it in a secure pocket inside my purse, I was inexplicably overcome by a sudden storm of emotion. Wracked by great sobs, I clung to Mother as it thundered around me while she enfolded me in her arms. She suddenly seemed so little to have borne the great burden of giving me birth and rearing me alone. When, like a summer shower, it rolled into the distance, we were cleansed, all past rancor and misunderstanding washed away.

"Thank you," I said at last. "Thank you for everything—for the sacrifices you must have made for me through the years. I wish you every happiness now—with Harve. You deserve.

"And for the ring. You, of course, know that I am not surprised to hear that it was my father's. I have always suspected it."

We emptied her dresser drawers into a suitcase. "I've missed having a father," I confided. "I think it was shameful of him to~"

"Don't blame him, Dear," she interrupted, pushing a strand of hair behind my ear. "Don't blame him. He never knew."

"Never knew?"

"No."

"I don't understand. Why didn't you tell him?"

"Well, I considered it but~"

"But what?"

"He had never told me he loved me. He was just comforting a lonely, miserable girl, and in our youthful ardor,~well~things got out of hand. Our passions burned out of control.

"Besides, I gathered from our conversations that his was a family of 'old money,'~wealth, culture, tradition~ Suppose he had married me, which he would have, had he known~to be honorable. His family would never have accepted me as an equal. I would have been the 'country bumpkin' in the family and would have been treated accordingly."

The answers only presented more questions.

"Why were you lonely and unhappy?"

"I'd been living with my father's sister, Aunt Olivia, and believe me, she wasn't easy to live with! She kept me under so much stress~ I was very unhappy there. Your father was a ray of sunshine in my life. But I knew~*we* knew it could never be."

"I'm amazed that a young person, such as you were at the time, would have the presence of mind to reason as you did. I doubt I would be as clear-headed as you were under the circumstances."

"O," she sighed, "I probably wasn't as clear-headed as it seems now. I would not have been able to articulate it then as I do now. I've had a lot of years to analyze the decision. It was an intuitive judgment, I guess. Something about it just didn't feel right."

"What did you do?"

"Well, I couldn't stay home. There were already too many mouths to feed. Aunt Belle was my only friend. She was dating Uncle Frank. She, of course, told him of my situation and he put me in touch with the Salvation Army. I was placed in a pretty good job since I had a Teacher's Certificate, and when it was time for you to be born, they took good care of us—you and me." She hugged me.

"Didn't they ask you for his name when you asked for help?"

"Yes, they were pretty insistent. But I was adamant. I knew that pressure would be applied. I also knew that such a marriage would not—could not last. There would have been heartbreak for everyone concerned, particularly you, and I wanted to spare you that."

I took a moment to weigh and appreciate that.

"Will you tell me his name?"

"No."

I knelt before her as she sat on the edge of the cot, and placed my head in her lap. We shared a brief shower of tears.

✳   ✳   ✳

Saturday dawned clear and blue, the kind of a day in June the poets have extolled since the beginning of time. Mother wore an Eleanor blue gabardine suit, a touted shade this year named for the new First Lady, and a matching wide-brimmed straw hat with lots of tulle piled on it to give it a bridey look. It was, after all, her first marriage. She carried a country bouquet.

Harve wore a *boutonniere* in the lapel of his pearl-grey suit. With his white wing-tipped perforated Florsheims and a blue silk tie that matched Mother's suit, he was handsomer than I had ever seen him. There were *boutonnieres* also for Uncle Frank and Dunbar and corsages of pink rosebuds and baby's breath for Aunt Belle and me. We were quite a *cortege* as we made our way into the courthouse that Saturday morning.

Dunbar and I were delegated to sign the Marriage Certificate as witnesses to the wedding, after which we posed for snapshots in front of the courthouse, Aunt Belle's Brownie 116 Kodak passing from hand to hand. As we walked to the parked cars, Harve gave Dunbar driving directions to the *Chateau on the Shore*, about fifteen miles north of the city, where reservations had been made for our celebratory dinner.

"Who's riding with me?" Dunbar wanted to know.

"Well," Harve said thoughtfully, "we all came together. You'll be riding all alone, won't you?"

"Yeah. Somebody can ride with me if they want to. How about you, Lindy? Would you keep me company?"

I hesitated. "Maybe we could all ride with you," I suggested. "Then the bride and groom could be alone together."

Dunbar's face became expressionless. "That's all right with me, if they want to."

It was plain that Mother wanted Aunt Belle to be with her. They looked at each other with uncertainty and embarrassment. Harve turned to me. "You wouldn't mind riding a few miles with Dunbar, would you?"

Taking my cue from the spirit of the occasion, I said "Okay, I'll be happy to ride with you."

Again I wondered why the obligation always fell to the youngest to make whatever concession a situation called for. Yet, I was eager to ride in his beautiful car. Black, in the conservative tradition, its chromium polished to perfection for the occasion, it sparkled like a bright jewel in the sunlight.

There was little conversation while Dunbar expertly maneuvered the car through downtown traffic. Breaking the silence after we were under way out on the highway, I asked, "What kind of car is this?"

"Oakland."

"It's a beautiful car."

"It *is* a beautiful car, isn't it?"

"I suppose it was very expensive."

"Hm-m-m, well--yes--somewhat. But then, if you want the best--"

As I watched the countryside slide past the windows, I was flushed with my fresh adulthood. I felt sophisticated, rich, even beautiful. KSEN had accepted my signature onthe contract as valid.

My first performance would be on Monday, the first week in July. The threshold was very real to me.

"I'm planning to buy a car."

He raised his eyebrows. "You *are?* Do you know how to drive?"

"Not yet. I'm going to learn."

"Who's going to teach you?"

I thought of Matt, but of course that was out of the question. "I don't know yet. Maybe Uncle Frank. I haven't asked him."

"Maybe he could teach you to drive his car. Then you'd be all ready to drive your own."

"Uncle Frank doesn't have a car. They sold it a few years ago."

"Would Harve be willing?"

"Gee! He has a brand new car. Although he might," I said, remembering that he'd been almost fatherly to me lately. "Anyway, I'm not ready to buy yet. I have to earn some money first."

"That's usually a prerequisite—money—for anything."

"How well I know! Besides, I need a few other things first."

"Such as—?"

"O, —" I hesitated. I wasn't going to tell him I needed a bed, some privacy, a place to shut the door. He was too remote from my life to confide in. Yet I felt obliged to answer.

He looked at me quizzically.

"O," I began again, "a lot of things—too numerous to mention." I laughed, trying to make light of it, but he wouldn't let go.

"What do you need?" he prodded. "I'm interested in hearing what it is you need."

I was becoming annoyed. I wanted to say *It's none of your business!* but I was intimidated by the circumstances.

"I haven't sorted it all out yet myself," I said deviously.

"When do you think you'll have it 'sorted out' ?"

"After I've seen a few paychecks."

"I might be able to help you fatten your bank account."

"I don't want to take on any more jobs right now," I argued. "What I'd like to do is get myself established in the one I have—sort of prove myself."

"Singing is not exactly what I had in mind."

"Oh?"

Dunbar made no answer as he drove, his eyes glued to the road ahead.

I shifted in my seat wanting nothing more than to be some other place when Dunbar abruptly turned off the highway onto a gravel road, stopped the car and turned the key. He put his arm around my shoulders and embraced me.

"Mr. Dunbar, this is ridiculous!" I heard myself say. I did not look upon him as a prospective lover. No one had ever propositioned me in this way before. "Just what do you have in mind?"

"In *mind?*" His voice was gentle, reassuring. "I have *you* in mind. Lindy! You're the freshest, loveliest thing I've seen for a long, long time. Kiss me!"

I was afraid. I pushed him away but he only strengthened his hold.

"Please, Mr. Dunbar!"

"Stop calling me *Mister*, dammit! I'm not your father."

Then, realizing that was the wrong tack, he changed his demeanor. "Lindy," he pled, "I want to give you all the things you've lacked—all the things you've been doing without. Why won't you let me? It's rough out there for a gal alone. You need someone to look after you. I could set you up in an apartment—pretty as you please—within a month—a week—a few days, if you wanted it."

I continued to press away from him, not quite knowing how to deal with this situation.

"Relax," he urged. "Just relax. Look at you! You're all tensed up. Don't you trust me?"

Trust him?

"I think we'd better get going," I countered. "We're going to be late. They're all going to be wondering what happened to us."

He didn't hear me. He was looking intently into my face. My breasts were tight against his chest. His brown fedora fell onto the floor behind as he planted his mouth over mine. I could not escape his hold despite my efforts. I felt his hand on my knee—then my inner thigh. An alarm went off in my brain, and with a surge of energy, I freed myself. Hurt and angry, betrayed, I slapped his face. Hard. I felt prickles at the back of my neck. Suppose I had angered him. What would he do?

I got out and let the door slam behind me only to find myself stumbling awkwardly on high heels as I tried to maintain my balance and my dignity on the gravel road which led to the highway. I really didn't know where I was going or what I would do. I just knew I had to get away.

I heard the car door slam, then the crunch of his footsteps on the gravel behind me. I envied him his flat-heeled shoes, for he quickly closed the distance between us with his long strides.

He walked beside me for a few moments, neither of us speaking.

"C'mon, Lindy," he said after a few minutes. He was flushed and contrite. "There's a better way to get there than this."

It was the best alternative available to me at the moment, so I walked back to the car with him. He quietly closed the door after me as I seated myself again. I hoped he didn't notice my hands tremble as I took a mirror from my purse. He watched thoughtfully as I rearranged my hat and refreshed my lipstick.

"You're wearing some of my lipstick," I notified him. "You'd better put yourself in order, too."

"That's not all I'd better do," he commented. He left the car for a few minutes and disappeared behind some shrubbery, while I drew a deep breath and composed myself.

After a few minutes, he retrieved his hat and again took his place behind the wheel. The tires spewed clouds of dust as the car snorted out of the gravel drive and backed onto the highway.

We resumed the drive in silence. He was driving too fast and once had to jam on the brakes to avoid a collision with a farmer's horse-drawn wagon which suddenly appeared in front of us as we came around a curve. He continued the trip at a normal speed.

Arriving at the *Chateau,* we found the wedding party already seated. Mother looked relieved as we walked in. There were questions in Harve's expression as he glanced at Dunbar.

"Where ya been?" he asked.

"Lookin' at the scenery," Dunbar answered.

"Musta been *some* scenery," Harve remarked.

"Beautiful," Dunbar answered, rubbing the side of his face where I'd slapped him.

I was blushing again.

Chapter 19

"Telepho-o-ne! Telepho-o-ne! Lindy-y-y! It's for yo-o-ou!" Aunt Belle sang it out in a lilting chant as it rang for the third time that evening after my first performance on the air. This time it was Bret.

"Hi, Lindy! Heard your show. You sounded good."

"Thanks, Bret. You helped, you know."

"Only a little. Feel like celebrating?"

"On a Monday night?"

"Why not?"

"I have to do it all over again tomorrow. Remember? And today was kind of an exciting day for me. Know what I mean?"

"Yeah, I guess I do. If I didn't have to work on the weekends— Tomorrow, maybe?"

"All right. Tomorrow," I agreed. I felt safe and comfortable with Bret—like family. He made me wish I'd had brother.

It seemed as though I had been standing in the back hall at that wall telephone for hours. I became aware of Stan, leaning over the banister upstairs, presumably waiting to use the phone. Earlier that evening, I had had a call from Marjorie. She'd heard the show, too.

"You seemed so composed, Lindy," she had said. "No sign of nerves at all. Were you really as calm as you seemed?"

"Well, I've done quite a lot of singing before this, you know. You helped me get started. Remember?"

"Yeah, I remember. Seems so long ago." There was a moment of reflection.

"How's your little one?"

"Almost nine months old already. Crawling around—pulling himself up on the furniture—getting into everything," she complained happily.

"How's your mother?"

Marjorie sighed into the phone. "She cries a lot."

"Cries?"

"Yeah."

There was silence for a moment. Not wanting to pry, I waited. Marjorie must have felt obliged to offer some explanation.

"You know, when I married Casey, I turned Catholic—and the baby—Timmy—was baptized Catholic. And my mother just broods about it all the time."

"How does your dad feel about it?"

"I can't tell. He doesn't say anything. He just listens—to her mostly. He adores Timmy—comes up to see him almost every day. I feel sorry for him. He's in the middle. I don't think he cares *what* we are."

After finishing my conversation, I called upstairs.

"Stan! Stan! You can use the phone now."

His footsteps sounded in the hall up stairs. "Geez! I better hurry up before the damned thing rings again!" he complained as he ran down the steps.

Mother, of course, had been the first to call, she and Harve having lately returned from their honeymoon at a resort somewhere in northern Wisconsin.

"We heard your show. You were good. I was proud of you."

"Congratulations!" Harve's gravelly voice intruded.

"Harve says your to come and have dinner with us after the show one day soon. When can you make it?"

"One day soon. I'll call you."

I was tired. Every night I had to wait for Aunt Belle and Uncle Frank to hear Everett Mitchell read the late edition of *The Chicago Tribune* from *WGN* at ten o'clock. The newspaper rattled as he turned the pages. Sometimes he even read a comic strip or two. *Skippy* or *The Katzenjammer Kids*:

"In the first panel, we see~"

"And the blurb says, ~"

Then we listened to *Amos 'n' Andy*. I would take my pillow and blankets out of the closet and make my bed, and every morning, as surely as the sun rose, the procedure was reversed.

The weeks flew by. The daily trip across town to the studio via streetcar and bus for rehearsals as well as performances, the additional time now required to maintain my appearance and my wardrobe, combined to make a long day.

The paychecks began to accumulate. I was somewhat intimidated by all this money, knowing what I wanted to do but fearful of getting in over my head. Suppose I was a flop? Suppose they terminated me at the end of my contract? Suppose I rented an apartment~the kind I wanted, with a real bedroom, which I could easily afford now~and suddenly found myself without a job?

I began perusing the ads in the newspaper looking for an apartment. I even rehearsed a speech I would give to Aunt Belle and Uncle Frank breaking the news of my leaving without hurting their feelings. It never occurred to me that perhaps they would welcome the privacy my presence deprived them of.

Then, early in autumn, two things happened which took the matter out of my hands.

Arriving at the studio at about one o'clock one day to rehearse in one of the studios which was not in use at that hour, I was advised by Sally, the receptionist, that Mr. Blackstone, the station manager, would like to see me in his office. Anxiously I opened the door which bore his name expecting to be in his presence. I found myself, instead, before his secretary in an outer office. A sign on her desk said *Helene Markowski*.

"I'm Lindy Albright," I said. "Sally told me Mr. Blackstone wanted to see me."

"Oh, yes, Miss Albright." Only slightly older than I, she had black hair, cut short and combed back in a poufed pompadour. She wore a white lace-trimmed blouse with a grey flannel skirt and dark-rimmed glasses. "I'll tell him you're here." As she rose to enter his office, I noted that she was heavier than her slender face indicated.

Mr. Blackstone, whom I had not met before, came to the door.

"Come in, come in," he invited me cordially.

A portly gentlemen, balding and taller than I, he wore silver wire-rimmed glasses. He was smiling as he gestured toward a chair opposite him as he took his place behind the desk. He wore a charcoal grey pin-stripe suit.

I seated myself gingerly and waited while he re-arranged some papers on his desk.

"Well, Lindy, have you read the reviews in the radio sections of the Sunday papers?"

"I sure have," I beamed. "I've even had some fan mail."

"Ye-es," he beamed. "We're aware of that. Quite a lot of mail. Well," he continued after a moment, "I think we have a sponsor for you."

"A sponsor?"

"Yes. It seems you're a favorite of Norm Zeitler who happens to be a distributor of candy and tobacco products here in the city. He's been putting pressure on one of his suppliers to sponsor your program. It will require that you begin and end your segment with a little theme which, I am sure, will give you no trouble at all. Otherwise, the format will remain the same."

With that he handed me the words and music for a four-bar beginning and a four-bar closing for the show.

White Owl Cigars! At first I was angry. I hated cigars! They stunk! But as I listened to Mr. Blackstone explain the terms of the contract and learned that my salary would triple, I reconsidered.

What the heck! I thought. *I don't have to smoke 'em.* In fact, I'd better *not* smoke 'em if I wanted to preserve my voice.

"Now," he said officiously, "I have a few papers here for you to sign. This will just take a few minutes."

He handed them across the desk to me. I glanced at the top sheet as I took them from him. As my eyes slid down the page, I knew that this would require some study. Mr. Rottman came to mind. I wished he were here. "When do you need my signature?" I asked.

"When? Why, the sooner it's signed, the better. I thought you might do that now. You can begin working at the increased salary as early as next week."

"I'd like to study the contract before I sign it," I told him. "I think my lawyer should examine it first."

"Your lawyer?"

"Yes, sir. I suppose I shouldn't say my lawyer. I've only seen him once. He examined the original contract--with KSEN."

"I see." He leaned back in his chair. The cordiality left him. He removed his glasses, then put them back on. "Well, there's nothing wrong with that," he said crisply. "I'm surprised, that's all. In times like these-- I just wouldn't expect a person your age to be so skeptical."

"I hope I haven't offended you," I almost apologized, "but I would feel better about it if he okayed it."

"Very well. You're welcome to do that."

As I rose to leave, he stood and shook hands with me across the desk and escorted me to the door of his office. Then standing in the doorway as I walked across the outer office, he called after me, "How long will it take to get an appointment with your lawyer?"

The secretary's jaw dropped as she exchanged glances with Mr. Blackstone.

"I'll call him now--from here. It shouldn't take more than a few days."

"All right," he smiled. "See you later."

I visualized the scene as the door closed behind me. Helene would be gasping, open-mouthed, "Why! The independent little brat!"

"Yeah," Mr. Blackstone would nod resignedly.

Of course, I only imagined it.

* * *

The good news bubbled inside all the way home. I could hardly wait to step off the streetcar at the corner. Bounding across the westbound traffic lane, I ran past the Schindler showroom and past the used car lot where Ray was dusting cars. In my exuberance, I smiled and waved to him as I passed. He waved shyly, as though I was a movie star or somebody great. He almost never spoke to me any more.

As I opened the door into the back hall, I considered how to spill the news so as to have the most dramatic impact. Uncle Frank was seated at the kitchen table, newspaper spread before him, while Aunt Belle was busy at the sink pouring top milk into a flowered pitcher.

"Hi!" I called from the hall as I breezed through the dining room into my closet to hang my coat.

"Hi!" they answered. Clearly, their mood did not match mine. I smiled as I walked back into the kitchen, but they weren't looking at me. There was a vertical crease between Uncle Frank's eyebrows. His mouth was unsmiling as his eyes perused the want ads.

"Whatcha lookin' for?" I asked while taking an apron off the hook on the pantry door.

"O-oh! Just lookin'," he answered.

Aunt Belle took a small roaster pan out of the oven. As she removed the lid, the steam rose filling the room with the salty scent of pork and onions. Peeled potatoes and carrots nestled alongside the golden chunk.

"What shall I do?" I asked.

"Get a platter," she said. "The one on the second shelf."

"Anything else?" I asked, handing it to her.

Uncle Frank put the paper aside and turned his attention to the evening meal. His expression didn't change.

"O, Aunt Belle, everything looks so good. And I'm so hungry. Mother was right! You are a genius in the kitchen."

"It's a nice kitchen," she said as she spooned the tastiest gravy in the world over her potatoes. "I hope the next one is as nice."

"The next one?"

"We're going to have to look for another place to live. This place has been sold," she explained.

This revelation pushed my news into the background. For a moment, I sat stunned.

"Mr. Justus came today to deliver our paycheck, and gave us notice," she went on.

"Oh! So that's why you're studying the want ads!" I said to Uncle Frank.

"That's why," he answered stoically.

There was little conversation during dinner, each having withdrawn into his own area of concern. I would not—*could* not—tell them tonight of my good fortune. They had just been dealt another blow. Being managers and custodians of that old rooming house had given them some status, at least among the tenants. It had elevated their morale and self-respect. It had been a job.

How could I tell a middle-aged couple—loved ones, at that—who have been down on their luck for years, that I, a nineteen-year-old, would now be paid a hundred-fifty dollars a week for fifteen minutes on the air five days a week?

I pondered Truth and Justice as it had been revealed to me by the philosophers whose works filled our high school literature and history books. I contemplated Marjorie's mother, Mrs. Van Allen and Casey and their opposing views of the *same* philosophy, but my deliberations provided no answers.

"We haven't wanted to come right out and ask you, Lindy," Uncle Frank said at last, "but we now have to know just what your plans are. If we have to look for a place large enough to accommodate all three of us, there will have to be some adjustment in the financial arrangement. You know there aren't many cars moving off that lot, and we've had not only free rent here but also some income. Now that's gone. We're right back where we started from."

"Well," I began, "I guess the time has come to tell you that I've been considering getting a place of my own. How much time do we have?"

"About six weeks. The new owner is taking over the first of October. We've been offered the Edwards' apartment upstairs. Erma and John have found what they think is a nicer place over on Washington Street."

"Do you think you'll take it?" I asked.

"We might. It would keep us close to Schindler's lot."

"It seems your problem is solved. I'm the one who should be looking at the ads," I said.

Aunt Belle cleared the plates from the table, poured more coffee and brought baked apples, sweet with candied sugar and cinnamon. We passed the flowered cream pitcher.

"I'm surely going to miss your cooking, Aunt Belle."

"We're going to miss you, too, Dear," she replied.

Chapter 20

"They're going to triple your salary," Mr. Rottman noted, peering mischievously over his spectacles from beneath his bushy white brows.

"I *know*," I answered, feeling naughty and guilty.

"How did your family react to this increase?"

"I was going to announce it triumphantly the other day, but things have taken a turn for the worse in their situation. I didn't have the heart."

"Smart girl! That was wise of you. No need to add to their misery."

I felt a need to confide. "I don't know what to do, Mr. Rottman." I blurted out the whole situation—about Aunt Belle and Uncle Frank—about the used car lot—about the rooming house being sold by the trust company—about Aunt Belle and Uncle Frank moving back into furnished rooms without having made any progress for all their work.

I told him about my needs—for a comfortable bed—some privacy—a place of my own—about my having nothing, my need to buy everything.

"I feel selfish," I said. "I want to help them, but I don't know how. They've been so independent—so proud. They don't want to accept anything—even from my mother. How would they feel about accepting anything from me?"

"You're entitled to your good fortune," he assured me. "You're entitled to be whole. You can't give of yourself unless you *are* whole.

"Go ahead," he urged. "Get yourself established in a home of your own. Provide yourself with what you need. Be alert to opportunities to be helpful and continue to watch over them.

"Remember, not all help takes the form of money. Just knowing you have some and that it's available to them is stabilizing."

"Do you think I should tell them about this increase?"

He thought about it a moment, then said, "I wouldn't be specific about the amount. You might tell them that you have a sponsor now, and that things are looking up for you. In that way, they will be assured that they don't have *you* to worry about. That's a gift in itself. It will do for now."

Our parting handshake was warmer and friendlier as we said goodbye.

"Thank you, Mr. Rottman. You've been very helpful."

"Your welcome!" he said earnestly. "And good luck!"

Before boarding the double 18 streetcar on National after leaving Mr. Rottman's office, I stopped at the corner telephone booth and called Mother.

"It's 'one of these days,'" I reminded her. "Is that dinner invitation still intact?"

"Sure is," she assured me. "What time can you be here?"

"I'll be through at the studio at six. Is seven o'clock all right?"

"Seven will be fine."

❋ ❋ ❋

It was a long ride via the city transit system, but it gave me thinking time. I had a strange feeling as I approached the address at which Mother lived. This was my mother's home—yet I had never seen it. She and Harve had rented an upper flat in a new duplex in an area which had begun developing just before the 1929 market crash. Harve had once talked about it at dinner before the wedding.

For months the whole subdivision project had lain dormant for lack of investors' money before the small savings bank which held the mortgage had risked finishing a few buildings.

The sidewalks were new. The streets were new. The street lights were of a different design than those I was accustomed to seeing in the old part of the city. Slender, willowy trees bent to the breeze in the parkway between the curb and the sidewalk. I remembered the huge overspreading chestnut trees which shadowed the walks where Matt and I had stolen kisses and experienced the first warm glow of desire. It would be a long time, many years, until these tender saplings sheltered eager lovers.

I found the number on a pale pink brick building with a porch across the front. A small neat lawn stretched across the lot. I touched the freshly enameled wooden porch with my fingers to be sure the paint was dry, then mounted the wooden steps and rang the doorbell. My mother's voice came from the tube.

"Lindy, is that you?"

"Yes," I called into it. "It's me."

"Okay," she said. "Come in."

A buzzer droned. I turned the knob and went in. The stairs were carpeted—a far cry from the blackened linoleum of National Avenue. I grasped the polished oak rail and looked up to see Mother smiling. We met with hugs and kisses at the top of the stairs.

Pervading the flat was the aroma of dinner cooking comingled with strong undertones of fresh plaster, paint and varnish. It was an uplifting, forward-looking smell—the smell of optimism—of beginning—of prosperity.

Harve came forward to welcome me. Extending his hand, he drew me toward him and kissed my cheek.

"Welcome to our home, Lindy!" he said.

"Thank you, thank you," I responded. "It's good to see you both again."

"Which would you rather have first?" Mother asked. "The dinner or the tour?"

"I'm starving!" I confided.

"Well, I see you haven't changed a bit."

Harve had hung my coat in a guest closet in the small hall at the top of the stairs. This done, we turned toward the the dining room.

As I looked about, hungrily soaking in all the details of the room, I was enchanted by the shiny china which was unfamiliar and new to me, the sparkling new silver on the fresh new tablecloth.

The chairs were new, the rug beneath our feet was new, its colors bright, its design intriguing. The chandelier over the table cast its warm glow over the scene.

"You're our first dinner guest," Harve advised me. "We may be a little clumsy as host and hostess. This is the first time we've worked together on such a project."

"Everything looks beautiful," I said. "I'll be your guinea pig anytime you want to practice."

"He's an excellent host," Mother told me. "He thought of a lot of things I would have forgotten."

"I *love* your china and silver," I said. "I suppose it was all very expensive."

Mother looked at me in dismay. The cost of things was hardly a subject for polite dinner table discussion.

"I'm sorry," I said, blushing. "The real reason I said that is because I'm going to be moving into a place of my own soon, and I have all these things to buy. I don't even know where to look, much less what to look for."

"Moving?" Mother said in surprise. "You haven't had a falling out with Aunt Belle or Uncle Frank, have you?"

"No," I assured her, whereupon I told her the whole story about the sale of the rooming house and Aunt Belle and Uncle Frank taking the rooms above the kitchen so they could stay near the Schindler used car lot.

"Where are you planning to go?" Mother asked.

"I haven't even begun to look for a place yet," I admitted. "A place near the studio would save a lot of travel time." It was the first concrete thought I'd had about it.

Now it was Mother's turn to break the rules. "Can you swing it? I mean, are you earning enough?"

"Yes, I'm doing very well. There's no need for you to worry," I said, remembering Mr. Rottman's advice.

✱   ✱   ✱

As August drew to a close, all eyes were focused on the calendar. October 1 was the target date. Erma and John Edwards needed only a week's notice before moving, since they had paid rent by the week. As soon as their apartment was vacant, Aunt Belle and Uncle Frank began to clean and rearrange it for their own occupancy.

I was getting up earlier these days to scout the neighborhood in the vicinity of the studio, newspaper in hand, for a suitable place to live. I remembered traipsing around with Mother while she did the same, and while I didn't actively participate in the decision-making process, I knew what questions to ask and how to evaluate the answers. I also had a pretty good idea of what to avoid. Moreover, Aunt Belle's experience in the rooming-house business was not entirely lost on me.

It was my original intention to avoid apartment buildings. The image in my mind was a composite of the little house Aunt Belle and Uncle Frank had had before the Depression hit them, Marjorie's cozy attic dwelling and Mother's new residence.

As I rode the streetcars and buses around the city, I saw many nice homes for sale. The newspaper ads, which I perused religiously these days, told me they could be purchased with what for me would be a small down payment, less than a month's salary! I wanted to remain more flexible.

I thought I found exactly what I wanted in an old home. The owners, a middle-aged couple who lived on the lower level, had also apparently experienced a downturn in their fortunes and had converted their expansive upper floor into a lovely apartment. It had heretofore been part of their one-family residence. I knew, as I grasped the curved, polished handrail and ascended the soft, blue-carpeted stairway that this was for me. We entered a furnished sitting room.

A tall striped wing-back chair caught my eye as it waited beside a small mahogany table. The sofa was upholstered in pink rose floral fabric. Mr. Rafael walked about the room as he talked, turning on the lamps which were scattered about. The carpeting was pearl grey.

We turned toward the bedroom at the front of the house. A huge poster bed jutted out into the center of the room. The long, shiny windows looked out over the regal old homes across the tree-shaded street.

As I turned from the view, I saw the corner fireplace. Faced with dark green tiles, it had a dark mahogany mantelpiece. I was at first amused as I recalled the lovely old marble fireplace in Apartment 4 on National Avenue.

"The kitchen and bath are back here," Mrs. Rafael said as she walked in that direction. I followed. The smell of fresh paint was pungent.

I liked it. It said *clean*. I sniffed and smiled.

"Is this for yourself?" she asked.

"Yes."

"You seem to be a very young girl to be looking for an apartment of your own. Are you married?"

"No."

There was a heavy silence for a few moments as they looked at each other—then at me, questioningly.

Again the lies chased each other around in my head.

"It's a convenient location for me," I volunteered. "I'm employed at KSEN."

"What do you do there?" Mr. Rafael asked.

"I sing."

"You sing? At KSEN?"

They looked at each other dubiously.

"I'm afraid we don't listen to the local stations as often as we should," Mrs. Rafael commented.

It was plain they didn't believe me.

"I've been riding streetcars and buses all the way from National Avenue. I would like to move in by October first."

"We-ell, I don't know," Mr. Rafael temporized, pursing his lips as he leaned back on his heels and contemplated the ceiling. "I have some misgivings about renting the place to a single woman—especially a *young* woman. Can you furnish references?"

"Why—no. I've never rented a place before."

I was about to tell them the whole story—about living with Mother—then with Aunt Belle and Uncle Frank—when I dug in my heels and decided I would not be coerced into confiding the intimate details of my life to total strangers.

I could see that both of them were full of questions—questions that good manners and proper up-bringing did not permit them to ask—but questions they wanted answers to, nevertheless.

"I really like the place," I ventured after a long silence. "If you'll take a deposit, I would like to move in as soon as possible."

"Would you be willing to pay forty dollars a month for it?" Mr. Rafael asked.

Mrs. Rafael registered surprise. The ad had specified thirty-five.

I thought a moment before I answered. I could easily afford it. I liked it. If there were any assurances that it would remain at forty—

"Would you agree to a lease?" I asked.

"A lease?" He looked to his wife for her affirmation. Her look told him nothing. "We hadn't considered a lease." He paced the floor for a few moments while we awaited his judgment.

"You understand, of course, that there are certain house rules we would expect you to honor."

"Rules?"

We couldn't allow, for example, your entertaining any young men except in the presence of a suitable chaperone—your mother, for example, or an older person."

"That's hardly practical," I protested. "My mother lives 'way across town. She has a home of her own."

They looked quizzical again. *Why wasn't I living with my mother then?* I looked around the lovely living room again and sighed. "Sorry," I said. "I've been a big girl for a long time."

The staircase did not look nearly as inviting to me on the way down as it had coming up. Mr. and Mrs. Rafael were behind me. As we arrived at the front door, Mr. Rafael said, "It's too bad we couldn't arrive at some agreement."

"Yes," I echoed lamely, "it's too bad."

I didn't know what they thought of me, and I didn't care. Tears burned behind my eyelids as I walked to the public sidewalk. It seemed that if my life didn't conform to an approved pattern, I would forever be barred from respectability or the enjoyment of the rewards of my talent, my earnings. I was odd. How had Matt's sister, Annette, said it? *A freak.*

Well! If the Rafaels of this world refused to grant me the privilege of being an emancipated person in charge of my own life, there were others who would. I now had more money than I needed, and no home unless I subscribed to certain *rules.* Hadn't I been practically self-supporting since I was seventeen?

When, after one of these search expeditions, I would return to National Avenue, I appreciated the fact that here, at least, I felt accepted.

I found what I was looking for at the top of the Hillcrest Hotel. The building featured a doorman and a large lobby where a desk clerk was on duty twenty-four hours a day. A dining room and coffee shop on the premises offered quick lunches, newspapers and magazines. Mr. Parkinson, the building manager eagerly whisked me up in an elevator and unlocked the suite which, he told me, had not been occupied for several months. He was obviously eager to get a paying tenant to correct this vacancy, a fact which I remembered when later we entered into negotiations for a lease.

I loved it! With its electric refrigerator~a bathroom and shower all to myself! A balcony! And two phones! What more could I ask?

The sight of the printed form brought Mr. Rottman to mind again. "I'd like to have my lawyer take a look at this before I sign it," I told him as we sat in his tiny office, now perfectly comfortable referring to Mr. Rottman as *my lawyer*. I smiled to myself.

"Of course," he said. "That's standard procedure for most of our tenants."

As I folded it into my purse, he leaned back in his chair and casually asked, "By the way, are you twenty-one?"

"No. I'm an emancipated minor."

"An emancipated minor," he repeated thoughtfully. "I don't think I've ever heard of such a thing."

"Well~" I hesitated, then began again. "Well, it means only that I don't live with my parents and I'm self-supporting. It means it's legal for me to sign my own contracts~that I'm responsible for my own debts~that sort of thing."

"In other words, you're an adult, is that it?"

"That's it."

"Hmph! Do you have any papers~any documentation to substantiate that?"

"No, I don't," I had to admit. "It's what my lawyer told me. I just accepted it."

"When you see your lawyer, have him prepare such a document for you~just a simple statement~and bring it with you when you bring the lease."

"All right," I agreed. It seemed a reasonable request.

The suggestion proved to be most valuable. Even Mr. Rottman admitted that he should have given me such a document on my first visit to his office. It became my most valuable possession during the months ahead before my twenty-first birthday.

Chapter 21

With my signature on the dotted line, events began to flow. September was already more than half gone, so from that moment, every minute not spent at the studio was given to pulling together what was needed to establish a comfortable home. Mother and I pressed Harve into service whenever we could since neither of us had learned to drive.

"I thought I was finished with this shopping business," Harve complained good-naturedly. "You women! You just want me along to carry packages."

"O, no, Harve," we cajoled. "We want your sweet company."

"My sweet *car!*" he would quip as he lifted himself out of his favorite chair and put on his jacket.

He was a good-natured chauffeur. Sometimes he took a book along and read in the car. He had no patience with domestics, but on the day we shopped for a bedroom set, he came along and offered good advice. While scrutinizing its construction, he questioned the materials, the durability of the finish, *et cetera.*

I was in an exhilarated state when they dropped me off at the studio. My dreams were materializing! A bedroom. A real bed. A home!

When I finished my show that evening, I was exhausted and planned to retire as soon as Aunt Belle and I finished the supper dishes.

"Did you get all your shopping done?" she asked as we hung the damp towels to dry.

"Most of it, I think." .

"What did you buy today?" .

"A bedroom set~and a spring and mattress."

"Aw-w-w!" she squealed, "I'm pleased. I've wondered how you endured that old daybed as long as you did. Nothing could make me happier than to know you have a comfortable bed."

"Thanks," I smiled. "I didn't want to talk about it because~well~ ~I wished things were going as well for you."

"Don't you worry about us!" she scolded. "It hasn't been a bed of roses for you, either. Uncle Frank and I want you to enjoy your good fortune."

I cupped her narrow, thin shoulders in my hands and turned her toward me. There were tears and hugs.

"Thanks. You've been the best aunt and uncle a girl could ever have."

In pajamas, robe and slippers, I lay down on the bare daybed to relax while listening to the evening programs, and promptly fell asleep. By the time Aunt Belle shook me awake to make up my bed, I had missed not only *Everett Mitchell* but also *Amos `n' Andy*.

❀   ❀   ❀

The next morning, I telephoned the manager of the Hillcrest to tell him packages would be arriving for me and to ask him what color the walls were in the bedroom.

"Since the place is unoccupied" he said, "pick up the key anytime. You can start bringing in your things."

"That would be very nice. Thank you."

When I turned from the phone, Aunt Belle was nowhere to be seen. After looking through the rooms, I called out, "Aunt Belle? Aunt Belle? Where are you?"

"Up here," she called. "I'm in seven." I walked up the stairs in the direction of her voice and found her on a small step-ladder adjusting a curtain on a rod.

"There!" she announced with satisfaction as she stepped down. "That looks a lot better."

She stood back from the window and viewed the crisp, starched, cotton priscillas as they covered the freshly polished window. The glass was wavy with age, the effects of blistering Julys and sub-zero Januarys through innumerable decades. At that moment, it did not matter that the view was of a dusty used-car lot below. Whatever went on outside these walls was of no consequence. Inside was cleanliness, warmth and love. It occurred to me that Uncle Frank and Aunt Belle were not as poor as I, in my naiveté, had perceived them. Indeed, they were far richer than I. They had each other.

I winced as the pain of loneliness stabbed me again.

❀　　❀　　❀

Since I was eager to decorate the bedroom, I stopped at the Hillcrest on the way to the studio to pick up the key. I would then go up to the apartment and check the color of the walls myself. I found Mr. Parkinson manning the desk when I later entered the lobby.

"Well, Miss Albright," he greeted me. "You came for the keys, did you?"

"That's right."

"We've taken the furniture out of that bedroom for you. The walls are green—light green."

I wrinkled my nose as I dropped the keys into my purse.

"The walls didn't look so good once the furniture was removed. I looked them all over. They're pretty well scarred up. We're going to do a paint job up there before you come in."

"That's wonderful! May I pick a color?"

"We-ell—within reason. Not black, I hope."

"No-o-o, although that would be beautiful, wouldn't it?" I visualized my creamy French Provincial bedroom set against the black walls—with black draperies featuring a huge creamy floral design, the soft glow of the vanity lamps~

"I really wasn't considering anything that drastic," I laughed, although the idea continued to intrigue me. "I'd like the bedroom to be light blue."

"That sounds okay. Light blue it is. The other rooms will be beige."

"Sounds fine. I'm getting excited about it now."

I arrived at the Hillcrest lobby at nine o'clock the next day. Nodding to the woman at the desk, I walked to the elevator, key in hand, feeling very proprietary. My purchases would be delivered this morning. As I walked toward my apartment, I noted the door ajar. I felt prickles at the back of my neck. Pushing the door open a crack, I peered inside. Then I saw the paint buckets and the ladder. Entering the apartment, I heard whistling echoing from the empty bedroom.

"Hello!" I called.

The whistling stopped.

I walked to the doorway. A man was spreading a tarpaulin on the carpet. He rose from a crouch as I came toward him. His eyes were as black as his mustache.

"How do you do?" he said shyly as he lifted his painter's cap. His hair, too, was black.

"Hello!" I answered, looking over the bare walls. "It's going to be blue, isn't it?"

"Yes. Blue."

We scrutinized each other for a long speechless moment.

"You look like the girl~"

"Are you Gloria's brother? Gloria Ruiz?"

"Yes."

"~and is this the tarp~"

"The same." He smiled and extended his hand. "Well, I'll be darned! Are you the lady~on Pierce?"

"Yes, I am. I tried to locate you~and Gloria, too. Couldn't find you in the phone book."

"How long ago, now?" He tried to remember.

"It must be about two years," I surmised. "I had just turned seventeen."

"You're nineteen now?"

"Yes. Nineteen." So Joe and I stood in the middle of this empty room, each full of questions.

"Tell me," Joe asked, "what are you doing here? How do you happen to be in this place?"

I laughed, because the answer was as unbelievable to me as it would be to him.

"This is my apartment," I said. "I'm going to live here."

His eyebrows rose in surprise. "O-o-oh! With your mother?"

"No, Mother's married now and has her own place."

"O-o-oh! She married that fellow—"

"Yes, she married him—just this past June."

I remembered my feelings toward Harve the night of the accident—how I'd rushed out of the apartment so filled with frustration and anger. I reflected on my changed feelings toward him. We were silent for a moment as we looked back.

The doorbell rang. My doorbell. It was the first time I'd heard it.

"Chapman's," the deliveryman announced as I opened the door.

I signed for the package which was clearly marked *FRAGILE-DISHES*. The deliveryman left.

"You're married?" Joe asked.

"No."

"You'll live here by yourself?"

A caution light flashed in my brain. I didn't really know Joe. How much should I reveal?

"I don't expect to be alone much," I extemporized. "I'll be having lots of visitors."

I had to change the subject.

The doorbell rang again. "Gimbels." Again I signed the

register. Another big package.

I wandered back into the bedroom where Joe had put up the ladder and was now on his knees stirring the paint for the ceiling. It looked pristine and beautiful in the bucket.

"How's Gloria?" I asked.

"She's fine. She's married now—keeping house—waiting for a little one."

"Is she happy?"

"I guess so. She looks happy when I see her."

"Both of you were so nice to me the night of the accident. I've always wanted to get in touch with you and thank you.

"We only did what was right."

"Yes, I know, but— Can you give me Gloria's phone number? I'd like to call her."

"Sure. It's HAnover 4121. She lives on Ninth and Washington." He had placed his bucket on the shelf of the ladder and was now climbing toward the ceiling.

"Ninth and Washington? I have a friend who lives in that neighborhood."

"Yes? Who's your friend?"

"Her name now is Orlikowski. Marjorie Orlikowski. It was Van Allen before she was married."

"Van Allen?" He wrinkled his brow, then dipped the wide brush into the bucket, wiping it at the edge, just so, and applied the first brush stroke to the dirty ceiling. A tiny light sparkled in the middle of my brain. I smiled despite myself.

"I think that's Gloria's neighbor. She has a little boy?"

"Yes, she has a little boy. Timmy."

"They get together for coffee every day."

We laughed in the spirit of two who shared a revelation.

There was one more delivery before I left. Pots and pans, and an ironing board from Schuster's.

"I really have to be on my way," I said at last. "Will you still be working here tomorrow?"

"O, yes. I'm going to do the whole apartment for you."

"I'll come by tomorrow. I have something for you."

"For me?" he pointed to himself, eyebrows raised.

"For you."

I left him poised on the ladder, paint brush in hand, as he puzzled over my remark.

After supper, I spent the entire evening rummaging through my drawers and closets looking for the scarf that Joe had placed under my head on the night of the accident. I found it at last among my sweaters which, of course, I had not worn since last winter.

In a spirit of mischief, Aunt Belle helped me find a box and some tissue paper, and together we gift-wrapped Joe's scarf.

When I arrived at the apartment the next day, Joe had completed the ceiling and was applying the lovely blue color to the walls. I was enthralled by the magic wrought by his brush and could visualize the finished room with my beautiful bedroom furniture in place.

"Here it is, Joe," I said as I held out the package to him.

"What's this? Some kind of a joke?" He came down the ladder and wiped his hands before taking the package from me. Carefully, he pulled the blue ribbon and removed the tissue. His black eyes opened wide as he recognized the scarf inside.

"*Caramba!*" Joe exclaimed. "My scarf!" He threw his head back and laughed. "*Dios Mio!* I forgot all about it. You kept it all this time? Thank you! Thank you! Gloria will be happy. She gave it to me for Christmas a couple years ago."

∾∾

Chapter 22

Delivery day for the bedroom set dawned at last. Mother was waiting in the lobby when I arrived.

"What's in the bag?" I asked as we walked toward the elevator.

"I brought something for our lunch."

She followed me in, uttering small exclamations of surprise and delight, and placed a jar of chili in the refrigerator. While we washed and arranged the new dishes on cupboard shelves, we waited for the call from the lobby notifying us that the bedroom set had arrived.

With Harve's cooperation, I had brought in most of my things. The fall apparel, which I was now using, was still on National Avenue. For the past week, I had been bringing in supplies. The *monitor top* refrigerator had milk and a few other necessary items in it, to say nothing of fascinating little ice cubes. Of course, this was *old hat* to Mother, who had a new electric refrigerator of her own. They were, however, a source of amusement and delight to me.

When at last the buzzer sounded, I was like a child on Christmas morning.

"It's here! It's here!" I exclaimed as I dashed to answer the intercom. "Yes--yes--I know--I'm expecting it," I answered. "Have them bring it up, please."

I rushed to one of the French windows, opened it and stepped out onto the balcony into the warm, sunny, Indian-summer day.

The fragrance of autumn was heavy in the quiet sunshine. The image of a yellow leaf on a chevron brick walk fleetingly brushed my consciousness and was gone. Looking down into the street below, I saw the top of the truck and a delivery man talking to the driver. The man got back into the truck, the bill of lading in his hand. They drove to a spot behind the building where they could access the freight elevator.

We watched as long as we could see them, and then lingered outside in the pleasant sunshine until we heard the doorbell.

"Albright?" the deliveryman asked, papers in hand.

"That's right. Right this way," I directed them toward the freshly painted bedroom.

"We'll bring the bed in last. You'll have to tell us where you want us to put your pieces. Gotta leave room for the bed."

Mother and I had a brief conference, quickly coming to agreement on where to place the vanity for the best light. Everything fell into place after that.

"It's even more beautiful than I remembered—and I've been thinking about it a lot."

"I'll bet you have."

When the delivery man appeared at the door with the vanity bench, I took it from him and carried it in myself.

Together they carried in my chest of drawers. I could hardly believe all that space was for me.

Finally, the *piece de resistance*, my beautiful bed.

"You really have gone without a lot, haven't you?" Mother observed. "I had no idea what a big price you paid."

"None of it matters now! It's behind me! And I've survived!"

"Still—" she worried.

"*Mother!* Black moods will not be tolerated in this house," I stated, establishing my territory. "Not today. Not any day. This is a *happy* day and I'm not going to let anybody spoil it by looking back!"

"*Well!*" Mother exclaimed and stalked into the kitchen.

The side boards had been placed while we talked. They came now with the box spring, all beige with blue roses, and set it in place. It looked comfortable enough to sleep on just as it was, compared to the lumpy old daybed.

"This is the last piece," the delivery man said as he backed into the room supporting one end of the matching mattress. They tipped it onto the box spring and *there it was!* A real honest-to-goodness double bed—big enough to stretch out and roll around on. *And it was mine!*

I smelled the chili and the coffee amid the rattle of dishes and silver. The delivery man produced the bill of lading for my signature. As I handed it back to him, he looked me straight in the eye and said, "Enjoy your new bed."

I stared at the closed door open-mouthed and red-faced.

"Lunch is ready," Mother announced from the kitchen.

I was in the bedroom. I had taken off my shoes and sprawled, face down, arms outstretched in an embrace of my new possession.

"How does it feel?" Mother asked from the doorway.

"Good."

"Do you want to sleep or eat?"

"I think I'll sleep," I teased, knowing I had to leave for rehearsal right after lunch.

"Would you like to make it up?"

"Yeah! Let's do that." I jumped to my feet, slipped into my shoes, and took the bedding from the closet shelf. "It's a shame to cover it up, it's so beautiful," I said as I tossed the mattress pad onto the bed.

With Mother on one side and I on the other, the job was too quickly done. I would have liked more time to relish the transformation.

The percale sheets were the snowiest white. Over them, a blue cloud of blanket, the soft wool, buoyant and alive under our fingers. Almost too precious to put to practical use were the white-on-white, hand-embroidered, hand-crocheted pillow cases, a gift of love from

Aunt Belle. For months I had watched her work on them during her leisure hours while listening to *One Man's Family* or some other radio drama. Neither of us knew then that they were to be mine.

Then the spread, blue, just a shade darker than the walls, of quilted taffeta graced by a crisp taffeta ruffle which extended to the floor.

"There! Now that's done," Mother stated with finality as she exited back to the kitchen.

To her, it was just another household chore; to me, it was an achievement. I was inclined to bask in the implications, but there was no dreaming with Mother around.

"You'd better get in here and have your lunch or you're going to be late," she ordered.

"Yes, Mother!" I answered with mock servility. Breathing a deep sigh, I acknowledged that she was right. Reluctantly I left the new bed to stand alone and unappreciated while I did what I knew I had to do.

The chili was hot and good.

"I'm going to sleep here tonight," I announced.

"But your fall clothes are still over at Aunt Belle's."

"I'll manage. Tomorrow morning, I'm going to move in. There's almost nothing left on National Avenue."

"I don't know if Harve will be free tomorrow."

"That's all right. I'll call a cab. From today forward, this is my address."

After the show that evening, I went *home*. Unlocking the door, I stepped into a dark apartment. The push of a button near the door brought light and reassurance.

Never before in my life had I spent the night alone. I turned on a lamp in the living room, just for company. Then lighting the kitchen, I busied myself warming the chili and coffee that was left from noon.

It was quiet, deathly quiet without a radio. I finished the chili, munched crackers, sipped coffee, found a piece of left-over coffee cake. There were also a few apples I had brought in a few days before. I ate one.

Mother had washed the dishes before she left the apartment, so I saw no need to bother with the few I used. I stacked them in the sink.

The phone would not be connected until the first. The newspaper I had brought home with me would be good company, but first I would take a bath.

Double-locking the door, I undressed and slipped into my old plaid flannel robe, then experimented with the faucets in the bathroom. There was a shower, but it wasn't usable tonight because there was still no shower curtain.

Imagine having a bathroom all to myself! I counted the number of people who shared one bathroom at the rooming house. Because I saw so little of them, I almost forgot about the people in Apartments 2 and 3 downstairs at the front of the building. When I added those five persons, one a child, there were fifteen. I marveled that we all stayed as healthy as we did. Then I remembered the strong smell of Lysol and chlorine when Aunt Belle scrubbed and cleaned, and her raw, red hands afterward.

Hot water! And it wasn't even Saturday! I rummaged through an unpacked carton for some bath crystals I had been given for my birthday a few years before. They had never been used. To luxuriate in a hot tub was an indulgence unthinkable where one bathroom was shared by fifteen people!

After my leisurely bath, I again put on my old bathrobe and made myself comfortable in an overstuffed chair under a lamp. The newspaper could not hold my interest. The novelty of the situation demanded my attention. The walls and the draperies clamored for inspection. The night scene from the windows fascinated me. As I moved from room to room, where the scent of fresh paint lingered, theambiance of my new surroundings penetrated my consciousness. I fantasized that it was opening to me and reflecting my identity.

Yawning, I turned out the lights and happily succumbed to the invitation of my lovely bed. The smooth buoyancy beneath me, the warmth of the blanket over my shoulders, was everything I had longed for. Lying on my back, hands behind my head, I looked up at the ceiling in the dark and allowed my body to sink into its comfort. Stretching luxuriously, catlike, I waited for sleep to overtake me. Instead, my mind was as busy as a hummingbird, darting from one thought to another. Half memory, half projection, people, incidents, plans, projects. Each idea spawned a dozen more. When I could no longer hang on to all of them, I dropped them and fell asleep.

Once during the night, I awoke, wandered through the rooms and looked down on the silent streets. Even at this hour, an occasional car moved along Shoreline Drive.

At last, my eyelids weighted with drowsiness, I went back to bed and fell into a heavy sleep. I dreamed I was being pursued. By whom? I didn't know, although the figure seemed familiar. Then I saw him. It was Bret. I was relieved. I stopped to wait for him, but as I watched, he was transformed. Before my eyes, he became Matt!--but not the same Matt I knew. He saw me without recognizing me. He drifted upward and took the hand of a woman somewhere in midair. She wore a white negligee. A raccoon coat hung loosely over her shoulders. They were gone! Still I heard the heavy breathing of my pursuer. I ran but got nowhere. Closer! Closer he came! His arms clenched my ribs. I awoke with a start as the last vibration of my own voice still echoed in my ears.

Dunbar!

જીજી

Chapter 23

December 5, 1933, saw the Twenty-first Amendment adopted at last when Utah, the thirty-sixth state, ratified. The date had been a memorable one, a day when even those who had never indicated any interest in alcoholic beverages felt compelled to enter into the spirit of *Happy Days Are Here Again,* the war cry of the Democrats at the last convention. The next day's newspapers were full of accounts of the misadventures of those who had imbibed too freely.

I had visited Aunt Belle and Uncle Frank in their *new* apartment that evening, and went with them to a freshly painted saloon, now known as a *tavern,* just a half-block up the street on National Avenue. We found all the tenants already there. They hailed us as we entered.

"C'mon over here," Stan beckoned us to their table while rearranging the chairs. Sitting with him was a plump, blond woman, near his age. She had red fingernails, long earrings, and a little too much rouge. Her eyes were glazed as she twirled between her fingers the stem of an almost empty "fish bowl," as the huge thirty-two-ounce glasses had been dubbed.

"This is Martha," Stan said shyly, somewhat embarrassed by his date's condition so early in the evening.

We shook her hand in turn, giving our own names. Since I was underage to be served anyway, I joined my Presbyterian aunt and sipped an orange pop. The others ordered beer. I was amused to see Uncle Frank struggling to get rid of a sixteen ouncer.

At an adjoining table were the Aldersons, Maggie and Jewel, along with Erma and John Edwards, who had walked the few blocks from their new address. Happy greetings were exchanged among people who knew and genuinely liked each other. We were happy to be together again. It seemed a celebration of the hopes and dreams we had for the future when we sat together and listened to the Democrats convention. Huge bowls of popcorn and pretzels were everywhere.

Dunbar and Harve now spent most of their time at the *Tux*. Mother would now be supervising waiters and waitresses at the new establishment, a number of whom had already been hired. Dunbar had purloined a chef from the Belmont Hotel on the Avenue and would be managing the bar and the bartenders, while Harve would concern himself mainly with matters pertaining to the real estate, building and grounds. With Mr. Rottman's help, they had formed a corporation and employed an accountant.

Final preparations were in progress for a gala Grand Opening on New Year's Eve. A temporary billboard had been erected on the site where the telephone number was emblazoned in foot-high red letters. Boldly it announced that reservations were available for the big event. Supported by newspaper ads and radio announcements, it generated sufficient response that I was pressed into service to answer the telephone. In the office, where I worked for a couple of hours each morning, carpenters scurried around me hammering the last moldings into place while electricians installed light fixtures.

This was the first time I had visited the site since that day last June when Mother and Harve had announced their coming marriage. The place then was no more than a hole in the ground. I was amazed and impressed with the size of the building and the glamour of the interior. Tables were in place around a parquet dance floor which, I was told by a workman, was laid over a cushion of cork. The Spanish plaster, currently in vogue and used throughout, was graced by ornate lanterns which emitted a golden glow. The ceiling was a replica of the open sky where stars twinkled eternally. Potted palms completed the illusion of a tropical night.

It was a stark departure from the reality of pre-holiday Wisconsin where the temperature was twenty-eight degrees when I left the apartment that morning. We had not yet experienced a heavy snowfall of the kind usually seen on New Year's Eve, yet there had been enough to create ridges where it was piled next to cleared sidewalks and roads.

The *Tux* had been, in fact, open for business since the first day of December, serving meals, soft drinks and three-point-two beer. Inasmuch as Schlitz, Blatz and Pabst were native to the city, and since repeal was expected to reduce unemployment and provide a market for grain, Wisconsin had no restrictive laws in place regarding the sale of liquor; therefore, all alcoholic beverages were sold immediately upon repeal.

I sat at the desk in the small office, alternately answering the phone and chatting with the workmen, when Dunbar poked his head in the door. A stubble of beard darkened his features. It was our first meeting since the wedding.

"Hi, Beautiful!"

"Hello, Mr. Dunbar," I answered respectfully. I imagined he could see my dream floating in a blurb above my head like a comic strip drawing. My face was hot again.

He ignored the *Mister* this time and strode into the room. His white shirt was open at the neck exposing the hair at the base of his throat. He leaned over me as he examined the reservation list before me.

"How're we doing here?" His hand rested on my shoulder as he brought his face close to mine. I felt prickles at the back of my head in response to his scent.

"Been listening to your show," he confided in my ear.

"You have?

"Yeah. You've got it, Baby. Think you could sing for us here sometime?"

"Here?

"Yeah. Here."

"Gee! I'll have to take a look at my contract."

He stood erect. "Who's your agent?"

"I don't have an agent."

"You're handling the deal yourself?"

"No. Mr. Rottman's been advising me."

"Rottman? How'd you get hold of him?"

"Through Harve."

"Good man, Rottman. He can't negotiate a price for you, though."

"I know that. He knows it, too. We've talked about it."

"What did he say?"

"Said he'd look into it if I wanted him to."

"Getting an agent for you?"

"Yes."

"Did he?"

"No. I never gave him the word. I thought I'd talk to you first. You might know of an agent. You hire Bret's orchestra. They must have an agent, don't they?"

"Bret's orchestra?"

"Well, the one he plays in."

He looked thoughtfully at me for a moment. "You know Bret pretty well?"

I shrugged. "Yeah. I see him once in a while."

"You like him?"

"He's okay, I guess. He's good company."

"Has he been up to your place?"

"Just to pick me up. We've gone to a movie a few times."

Dunbar nodded.

"I hear you've got a pretty nice place."

He was onto my favorite subject. I waxed enthusiastic.

"I love it! It's beautiful." I almost told him about my luxurious bedroom—for it seemed that to me—but caught myself before I spilled it.

"I'd like to see it sometime."

"I've been thinking—I should have a little party. I owe a lot of people."

"That's a good idea. Trouble is, I don't know when I can get away any more. Your mother and Harve are going to be tied down, too."

Until now, I had not considered how restrictive the business would be to their activities.

"Will you be open on Christmas Day?" I asked.

"Not until five o'clock."

"I could manage a brunch, I think."

"A Christmas brunch? Great idea! I'll be there!"

"Hey, wait a minute! I haven't decided yet!"

"I'll be there!" he said, laughing.

"Hey, what about the agent?" I called after him, but he was gone.

That's how it happened that, like it or not, I was committed to hostess a Christmas brunch with about two weeks to plan it. I'd never even participated in such an event and didn't even know anyone who had.

After the show that night, I stopped at the coffee shop just off the lobby for a hot beef sandwich as I'd done on a few previous occasions. The cook was manning the cash register this evening while the cashier enjoyed her dinner in a back booth since the rush hour was now over.

"Enjoy your meal?" he asked as I fumbled in my purse for my wallet. He was middle-aged, with pitch black hair and a large nose. He had a Semite look about him—maybe Lebanese.

"Sure did. It was delicious. Maybe I should hire you for my brunch," I said laughing as I handed over the cash.

"Brunch? You gonna have a brunch?"

"I'm afraid so. All I did was mention the possibility and somebody jumped on it. Now I'm committed and I don't know *anything* about planning a brunch."

"It's easy," he said, gesturing with a flaccid hand. "All you do is~"

For the next two or three minutes he expounded on the proper way to to prepare ready-mix pancake flour into waffle batter~make a vat of coffee~buy a crate of juice oranges~squeeze a vat of juice~put five or ten pounds of sausages under the broiler~a couple pitchers of syrup, preferably maple, *et cetera, et cetera.*

"Mr. ~," I interrupted his desertation.

"Herman," he filled me in. "Just call me Herman."

"Okay, Herman. You make it sound so easy. You don't seem to understand, I don't know how to do any of these things very well~even for myself. To get it all together for a crowd of people~"

"How many people?"

"Well, let's see." I began counting on my fingers. "Mother and Harve, Aunt Belle and Uncle Frank, Marjorie and Casey and the baby, if they'll come on Christmas Day. I'll have to call her. I'll have to call them all. Bret, Dunbar~ How about Stan? If I invite him, I'll have to invite the Alderson's, too~Maggie and Jewel. Well, why not? I'd like to have Joe and his sister, Gloria, and she has a husband now~ How many is that?"

"I count fourteen~plus you is fifteen. You got room for that many in your apartment?"

"I can accommodate eight in the dining room and four in the kitchen. Maybe I could borrow a card table somewhere~set it up in the living room."

"Say no more. I can get you an extra table. Which apartment are you in?"

"The top one."

"The top one?" He was impressed. "How big is the living room?"

"Pretty big. It will accommodate a table and some folding

chairs. Say, Herman, you're a big help. You're helping me think through this thing."

"I'd be glad to help you if you want me to," he offered.

"O, Herman, I couldn't ask it of you on Christmas Day!"

"Is that when you're gonna have it? Christmas Day?"

"That's the only time some of these people can get away. They're in the same business you are."

"That so?" he asked. There was no one around now. He was preparing to close as we talked.

I told him about the Tux. He had heard of it--heard the ads on the radio. He was impressed.

"Christmas Day don't mean nothin' to me," he said. "It would give me somethin' to do--someplace to go."

"You're serious?"

"Yeah. Sure, I'm serious. I'll get it all ready for you. I got a kid, George, son of a friend o' mine. He helps me out once in a while. He won't mind. He'll be glad to earn a couple o' bucks."

"Don't you have a family, Herman?"

"Na-a-ah! Someplace, I guess. I sure as hell didn't grow on a blackberry bush. But my family's scattered. I never got married myself. My sister, she's back East--married--with kids. I never hear from 'em."

"Gee! That's too bad." I commiserated with him. "If that's the way it is, I want you to know that I surely would appreciate your taking this thing off my hands. Herman, I don't even own a waffle iron. Should I buy one? What kind should I get?"

"Na-a-ah! I'll bring one up from here," he waved toward the kitchen. "And, hey! Maybe you could get some champagne from the Tux?" He brought his thumb and forefinger together and grinned wickedly. "That would be a nice touch!"

"Herman! You're a genius! This could be a real bash!"

"It could."

∂∂

Chapter 24

A few days before Christmas, the house phone buzzed as I enjoyed a leisurely breakfast at my kitchen table. I was told that a man with a Christmas tree wanted permission to bring it to my apartment.

"A Christmas tree?" I asked, puzzled. "Who's the man?"

I heard the desk clerk ask, "What's your name? She wants to know who it is. Dunbar? The fellow says his name is Dunbar."

I was stunned into silence for a moment.

"Hello? Hello? Are you there?"

"Yes. I'm just thinking."

"Should I send him away?" the clerk asked confidentially.

"Damn!" I muttered to myself. I wasn't even dressed. "Tell him to wait fifteen minutes."

I finished my coffee, and went into the bedroom to dress—and make the bed! Dunbar was not a man to be given any suggestions or opportunities.

I had barely had time to pull a comb through my hair when the doorbell rang. When I opened the door, all I saw was the tree, bushy and green, its pungent pine scent filling the room. I spotted a pair of big wet boots making puddles in the hall, and through the branches, like a Christmas decoration, a red wool cap.

"Come *in!* " I scolded. "You're dripping all over the hall."

"Ain't she a beauty?" he grinned, turning it so I could admire its symmetry.

"Dunbar! You didn't find it in a park, did you?"

He leaned back in a hearty laugh. "Hell, no! I came by it legitimately. Thought it might be a nice touch for your Christmas party."

"But Dunbar," I protested, "I don't have a thing to put on it. Not even a stand."

"Don't worry about a thing," he assured me. "Where can I set this thing while I go down to the car. I've got a stand."

Hastily, I pushed a few pieces of furniture aside and made space for the sprawling tree. While I stood admiring it, fondling its branches and reveling in its lovely fragrance, he returned with a large cardboard carton.

"There's more," he said as he left to go back to his car.

As I leaned over the box, he shouldered the door open and brought in another carton. It tinkled.

"What's that?" I asked.

"The champagne."

"My goodness! How much did you bring?"

"A case. Twelve bottles."

"Whatever am I going to do with twelve bottles?"

"It'll go. You'll see. Did you ever taste champagne?"

"No."

"You'll like champagne," he said, while presumptuously taking off his boots and laying his coat and cap on an overstuffed chair. Then he got to his knees and began to unpack the carton.

I made no comment. I hated drunkenness. Still, I had tasted wine when I sang at weddings. I was uncomfortably on the fence on the issue.

At the top of the carton were boxes of ornaments, packages of tinsel, and lead foil icicles. Uncle Frank had always called it "rain."

Next came the lights. A half-dozen strings of lights—overflow, I suspected, from the mammoth purchase he must have made to decorate the Tux for the Grand Opening. Finally, down at the bottom, was a metal stand, a rather ingenious device which held the tree in position and allowed it to stand in water.

He lifted the tree into the stand. "Now," he ordered, "you hold it straight and steady while I turn the screws."

"All right," I agreed, wondering at my own unquestioning obedience. I stood and held. And held. I couldn't see what he was doing at the bottom of the tree. My arm was getting tired. Why was I doing this? Just a few minutes before, I had been sitting at my own kitchen table savoring my breakfast and my solitude, and now here I stood, my arm aching, taking orders from Dunbar.

"It's listing a little to the south."

To the *south?* "Which way is south?"

"That way."

He must have pointed. I couldn't see him through the thick branches.

"Not that way," he said impatiently. "the other way. Opposite."

"*Okay.*" My voice held a belligerent edge. I pulled it in the other direction.

"No-o-w, just a *le-ettle* bit more," he coaxed. "There!"

"Can I let go now?"

"Sure, you can let go."

I rubbed my aching arm as I let it fall to my side. "*Ugh!* I'm glad that's over."

With the tree established, Dunbar warmed to his project.

"Now the lights. Let's see. Where's an outlet? I brought an extension cord."

This was not how I had planned to spend the morning. Sitting on the sofa, I watched him open the boxes. I got down on the floor and helped him straighten the wires where they were tangled. He became an oversized boy having the time of his life.

"Will you have a tree at your house?" I asked.

"Na-a-h!"

"Who trimmed the trees at the Tux?"

"We had a decorator come and do it. And I guess your mother helped."

"Did you have nice Christmases when you were a kid?"

"Yeah. Pretty nice. My father had a saloon. I don't remember much of my mother except she was pretty. My dad tried to make up for it. He'd buy me lots of toys. I was the youngest—the baby."

He plugged in the lights as they lay in a cluster on the floor. The brilliance of the colored bulbs ignited the Christmas spirit within me. I gazed at them entranced.

Dunbar's eyes glazed over as he, too, became enchanted.

"What happened to your mother?"

He turned to pull the plug out of the wall socket, and began putting the lights on the tree. I got up to help.

"There was an accident." I listened while I watched him distribute the lights, helping where I could.

"There were seven of us in my father's car. It was an open touring car. An Overland, I think. My father was driving."

He paused to stand back and evaluate what he'd done.

"It was night. We kids were all talking and making a lot o' noise."

The lights were in place on the tree. We dug into the ornaments—all silver and gold and red and green and blue, he on one side and I on the other.

"We didn't hear the train whistle. There were no lights at the crossing—just a crossbar on a pole. It said *Railroad Crossing*."

We draped the tinsel, handing the bundle from one to another as it went around and around.

"When they picked up the pieces, my mother was dead. Thrown through the windshield. Later, my sister died, too. Three of my brothers were in a hospital, one for a long time. My father got out of it with only minor injuries. I had a broken leg—hobbled around on crutches for—I don't know—six or eight weeks. In a cast. I was a celebrity among the kids on the block for a while."

"How old were you?"

"Seven."

"You were old enough to suffer."

"Yeah." His voice was husky. He pulled a handkerchief from his back pocket and blew his nose.

By sheer force of will, he changed his demeanor. "Look at that tree!" he exclaimed. "We're almost finished. Let's get at the icicles. Is there a good place to eat around here? I'm getting hungry."

"There's a coffee shop downstairs."

"I was thinking about something nicer than a coffee shop," he said, "but I'm not really dressed to go to a good restaurant. How's the menu down there?"

"Good! Simple fare, but well prepared. I sometimes eat there after the show."

"Okay. Sounds good. We'll have lunch together. Okay?"

I consulted my watch. "It's about all I have time for. I have to leave for rehearsal."

We had put the finishing touches on the tree during this exchange. Lying prone, Dunbar pushed the tree into position in front of a long window which opened onto the balcony, then plugged in the lights. It was a vision! We both stood back and admired our handiwork.

"Ya know," he beamed, "this is the first Christmas tree I ever trimmed!"

"Me, too."

"For a couple of amateurs, we did all right. Wouldn't you say?"

I felt his arm around my waist. "Yeah, I'd say," I answered, smiling while resisting as he drew me toward him.

"Just one? For Christmas?" his eyes pled.

"Okay," I agreed. "Just one."

As our lips met, the memory of the dream crept into my mind. His maturity, his manliness, the stubble on his chin, awakened in me the longing I had been denying and suppressing for~how long? Forever, it seemed.

"Are you going to give me the tour?" he asked, still holding me.

"The tour? Oh! You want to see the apartment."

"Yeah," he said, kissing me one more time before he released me. Looking around for the first time, he said, "This is pretty nice, what I've seen of it. Is this your own furniture?"

"No. It belongs to the Hotel. I intend to replace it with my own—gradually."

"This is a comfortable arrangement," he said. "I like the openness of the living-dining room—no separating wall. It has a feeling of spaciousness."

"I like being at the top of the building. There's a phone here in the alcove."

"Quite a distance to run—isn't it—to answer the phone? Suppose you're in another room?"

"There's another phone in the central hall."

"Two phones! Talk about class!"

At that moment there was sublime gratification in the fact that I had been able to provide well for *myself*, without any help from him, all the things he had offered me at the time of Mother's wedding.

We walked through the central hall which accessed the kitchen, the bathroom and the large bedroom at the other corner of the building. A smaller bedroom was tucked in behind the bathroom and beside the large bedroom. I had done nothing with it and had no plans for its use.

As we went from room to room, he made favorable comments, helped himself to a drink of water at the kitchen sink.

"Now, this is my own furniture," I said with pride as I stood at my bedroom door.

"Hmm! French Provincial! The lady has good taste!" He stepped inside and examined it approvingly. "It looks like a lady's boudoir."

"How would you know it's French Provincial?" I teased.

"We-e-ll," he stalled, "a fella gets to know about such things." Chuckling, he extended his arm around my waist, drew me toward him and, with a wicked wink, kissed me again.

Chapter 25

Christmas Eve fell on Sunday this year giving me two free days before the brunch. Marjorie had called and gleefully announced that they would be able to come, which meant another gift to buy for Timmy. I found myself among the last-minute shoppers despite my early efforts to avoid the crush.

As I pushed past a crowded *Men's Furnishings* on my way to *Toyland*, I looked up into a familiar face. So out of his customary milieu was he that I had to search my memory for a moment before I could identify him.

My English teacher!

"Mr. Richmond!"

"I know the face," he responded, "but the name escapes me. No! Don't tell me. Let me think. Lindy, isn't it? Lindy Albright?"

"You remembered!" I gushed. I was flattered.

"Doing a little last-minute shopping?"

"Yes, a toy for my friend's little boy. What do little boys like?"

"I wouldn't know. It's been a long time since I've been one."

"Do you have any children, Mr. Richmond?"

"No." The smile disappeared. "The marriage never took place. The engagement was broken."

I was astounded that he would make such a confidential statement to *me.* He could as easily have said simply, *"No."*

"I'm sorry to hear that."

"Yeah. Makes for kind of a lonely holiday season. Do you have a family?"

"Of sorts."

We had been blocking the passage of customers through the aisle and had moved into a corner where we would be out of the flow.

"Of sorts? What does that mean?"

"Well, my mother is married to a man who is not my father."

He shrugged. "Nothing so terribly uncommon about that."

"No, I guess not. He's a good person, I guess."

"Any sisters or brothers?"

"No. But lots of friends. I'm having them all as guests at a brunch on Christmas Day."

"That's great. Glad to hear it. You've got a boyfriend, I presume."

"No, no one special."

"I'm surprised. Well, have a good time," he said, placing his hand on my sleeve as he turned to leave. "Merry Christmas!"

"Why don't you come?" I heard myself say almost involuntarily.

"I couldn't impose on you."

"No imposition, really. There will be about fifteen of us. One more won't be noticed. We're going to have waffles and sausages."

"Waffles and sausages, eh?" He smiled displaying his strong, even teeth.

"And champagne."

"Champagne! Lindy! You have grown up, haven't you? You make me feel like an old man!"

"Do come," I urged him.

He was considering, I could tell.

"Where is it going to be?" he asked at last.

"I don't have any cards, but I can write it down for you." Nervously self-conscious, I scrounged in my purse while he calmly withdrew an envelope and a pen from his inside jacket pocket and wrote down the information.

"That's a pretty classy address, isn't it?" he observed.

"Well,~" How do you tell your former teacher that you're earning more money than he does? "I've been lucky! I'm singing at KSEN. I have a sponsor~"

"You're *Lindy?*" he asked incredulously.

I nodded.

He smiled. "Well, good for you!"

I looked at my watch. "I really must get that toy!" I exclaimed. "Will you come?"

He stood looking at the envelope in his hand. "Eleven o'clock, eh?" There was a half-smile on his face as he regarded me. "You make it sound tempting, Lindy. I'll think about it." He tipped his hat to me as I hurried toward the toy department.

I was in an elated state as I entered Toyland. To think that Mr. Richmond might~just might~honor my brunch invitation made me feel~*worthy*. I had always categorized him as a "quality person," a man of intellect and sensitivity.

I found the toy department pretty well picked over this close to Christmas, particularly since this would be a better Christmas for many than it had been for a long time.

Since Timmy was now about fourteen months old, he would be walking. A pull toy would be in order. I found a wooden train consisting of an engine, a box car and a caboose, all painted in bright, primary colors.

❉ ❉ ❉

I selected a forest-green dress of sheer wool for the brunch. It featured the V neck and wide shoulders which were so fashionable this year. Gored from shoulder to hem, it was narrow at the waste and full skirted. A stand-up collar tapered to nothing at the point of the V. I accented it with bright red, chunky costume jewelry. My earrings were tiny glass Christmas-tree ornaments.

I had set the alarm for 6:30 a.m. so that I would be bathed and dressed before Herman and George came ringing my doorbell. At about 7:45 they arrived, pushing two-shelved cart before them. On it was the restaurant coffee urn, a huge waffle iron which turned out four waffles at a time, orange juice, waffle batter, *etcetera*.

I had set the tables the night before after wrapping Timmy's gift.

"What kind of weather are we having?" I asked Herman.

"Cloudy, we're gonna have some snow later on, I think. But the streets are dry. They shouldn't have any trouble getting here."

"How about getting home?"

"Never can tell," he answered. "I wouldn't worry."

By 10:45 everything was humming. I smelled the coffee brewing as I poured orange juice from a glass pitcher into the glasses on the table. As the sausages browned under the watchful eye of George, Herman baked waffles. He lifted them from the iron, then placed them on a large cookie sheet and placed them in the oven above the broiler. He had accumulated quite a stack.

I was beginning to worry that nobody was coming when the doorbell rang giving me a start. First to arrive were Mother and Harve. Mother carried an apron.

"Just in case you needed some help," she offered.

There were hugs and kisses and Merry Christmases all around. By the time I had taken their coats, Aunt Belle and Uncle Frank came in and we went through the same ritual.

"O, Lindy! This is lovely. I'm so happy for you."

"Thanks, Aunt Belle. I'm really enjoying it."

"Yeah, pretty nice. Pretty nice," Uncle Frank agreed.

Then Bret greeted me with a hug and a kiss. He gave me a gift-wrapped box. I blushed and unwrapped the box of Fanny Farmer candies.

When I heard several voices at the door, I knew it was Marjorie, Casey and the baby along with Gloria and her husband, whom I had never met.

"Merry Christmas!" rang out from all of them as Gloria and I embraced. We had not seen each other since the night of the accident.

"How nice of you to ask us to come! What a fancy place you've got here! Boy!"

"I'm glad you could come."

"This is my husband, Ricki."

"How do you do."

Bret came to my rescue and helped with the coats. There were cross-introductions all around.

"I look different, eh?" Gloria smoothed her dress over her pregnant belly.

"Yes. Some*what.*"

"Not for long. Pretty soon it'll be gone and I'll hold it here," she said, making a cradle of her arms.

Bringing up the rear was Joe.

"Felice Navidad!" Joe exclaimed as he came through the door smelling of cold fresh air and after-shave. "Look! I wore the scarf today. In your honor. See?"

"I see," I laughed as Marjorie handed the baby to me. He was a heavy little fellow, especially bundled as he was in a snowsuit and galoshes.

"Just hold him a minute while I take my coat off," she said.

"I don't know if I can. He's heavy.   Does he walk yet?"

"O, yes. He's been walking for~" she turned to Casey, "about two months now, isn't it?"

"About that," her husband answered.

"I think I'll let him stand," I said, setting him on his feet. "Hi, Timmy! What a big boy you are!"

He looked at me soberly with wide, blue, questioning eyes.

"There's a little present for you under the tree."

"O, Lindy! You shouldn't have."

The door was still open when Stan came in followed by the Alderson ladies. He carried a white paper bag. "Merry Christmas!" he said. "Here's a little something for you."

I peaked inside. A *Whitman's Sampler.* Five pounds!

"I brought Jewel and Maggie. They're right behind me."

"Merry Christmas!" they chimed together. They were both

bejeweled, rouged and lipsticked to perfection. Smiling and nodding, they were obviously ill at ease in this strange environment.
This was an adventure for them both. Each of them carried a small
tissue-wrapped package which they pressed into my hands as I
helped them with their coats. Inside were hand embroidered linen
handkerchiefs with tatted edges, each of which represented many
hours of patient, skillful work.

"O, thank you! thank you! All of you. I really didn't want you
to bring gifts. I'm embarrassed, really."

Jewel squeezed my hand and with tears almost spilling over, she
hugged me and whispered, "Make the most of it, Dearie. Make the
most of it! You're only young once." I hugged her and permitted
myself a moment's reflection on her restricted life.

They really filled the apartment. I had not even finished taking
their coats when Dunbar appeared. He wore a navy pin-striped suit
with a blue silk tie and had quite obviously *dressed* for the occasion.
A large diamond flashed from his ring finger.

Confusion reigned for a while as I made introductions all
around. Picking up snatches of conversation, I overheard many
favorable comments about the apartment. I heard Gloria extolling
the beauty of the tree to my mother while Dunbar revealed to all
present his participation in bringing it about.

Bret sat on the floor and busied himself helping Timmy
unwrap the train. Dunbar was Bret's boss in a round-about way.

I consulted with Herman. Everything was ready to serve.

"What time is it?" I worried as I looked at my watch.

"About ten after eleven."

"I'm kind of waiting for one more guest. Can we stall a few
minutes?"

"Well, it'll take ten or fifteen minutes to serve all these people.
She might come while we're doing that."

"Yes—ah—well—ah—it's a man."

"So? He'll come. Or he won't. I'd like to get started. Okay?"

"Okay. I'll get everyone seated."

"George," Herman said, "did you bring that high chair?"

"Yeah. It's in that little bedroom. I'll get it."

"You brought a high chair?"

Yeah. You mentioned there might be a baby."

"And you remembered?"

"Yeah."

"Herman! You're unbelievable!"

I went back to the living room. "You may find your places at the table," I announced. "You may not be sitting with your spouse except for Marjorie and Casey. They have a little responsibility to manage between them."

I wonder if he'll come, I thought as everyone looked for his own name on the little cards I had placed at each plate. The doorbell rang again.

It's him. It's *he!* I corrected myself, then laughed. Why was I so excited? Wouldn't Marjorie be surprised? I opened the door.

He carried a long green box.

"Come in, come in! I'm so glad you decided to come. You're just in time. Let me take your coat."

"For the hostess," he said.

"For me?"

"For you."

I opened the box under the curious stares of everyone in the room. "A *rose!*" I exclaimed.

"A *rose!*" breathed every woman in the room.

While Herman and George brought in platters of waffles and sausages, the rose passed from hand to hand as each inhaled its lovely fragrance. Roses in December were a rare experience in our part of the world.

Lacking a tall vase, I settled on a tall glass and placed it on the dining room table.

"O, my goodness! I haven't introduced you," I apologized. There was so much conversation, I had to rattle a spoon against a glass.

"I'd like to introduce Mr. Richmond, who was my teacher of English and English Literature in high school. I think he was Marjorie's teacher, too. Wasn't he, Marjorie?"

"Yes, I remember. What a surprise to see you here!"

I then recited the names of everyone there knowing he wouldn't remember half of them although they would all remember him.

The champagne had been poured and we were all at last seated and ready to begin enjoying our meal when Harve proposed a toast.

"I think Elsa Maxwell had better look to her laurels if she expects to continue to be known as 'the hostess with the mostest.' She has a rival right here in our midst."

"I'll drink to that!" Joe said, raising his glass. "Merry Christmas!"

"Merry Christmas!" we all said together, and sipped our champagne.

"It wouldn't be fair to take all the credit," I said as I rose from my chair. "Herman! George! Come out of the kitchen for a toast."

Shyly they appeared while we raised our glasses again.

"Here's to Herman and George!"

"Merry Christmas!" we all said together.

Chapter 26

Amid the hum of conversation, the platters were quickly emptied, as were the pitchers of orange juice and the glasses of champagne. The sun broke through the clouds occasionally bathing the scene with its anemic, solstice light which was at once comforting and depressing. Its heat, coming through the glass, created currents of air which caused the foil icicles on the tree to sway and rotate, giving it a living presence.

I was appalled by the quantities of food consumed as Herman and George brought in the replenished platters. I again filled the glasses with juice while Dunbar took it upon himself to pour more champagne.

"Joe," Gloria admonished her brother from the living room, "you be careful you don't drink too much. You have to drive us home with a baby in the car and another on the way."

"Don't worry about me. I can take care of myself," he answered in typical brother fashion.

I hoped Dunbar would take the cue and refrain from pouring any more champagne.

"I'm a little concerned about over-indulgence this holiday season and the accidents which might result," Mr. Richmond commented, little knowing that Harve and Dunbar were indebted to the dastardly *witches brew* for their livelihood.

"I think prohibition was a good law!" Maggie, equally ignorant of the circumstances, said with conviction. "Better to give the grain away to the starving people in the world we're always hearing so much about than to make booze out of it."

Aunt Belle, sitting across the table from her, nodded almost imperceptibly but said nothing. I knew she felt the same, but in deference to my mother and Harve, felt it wise to let others carry the banner into the fray.

"Well," Harve argued, demonstrating his brash irascibility, "would you rather have people drinking 'bathtub gin' and going blind? That's what we've had up to now. At least now the stuff is made under regulated conditions."

"People who want to drink are going to drink whether it's legal or not," Casey offered. "I'm for lawful distilling of the stuff myself,"

"A little is all right, I guess," Marjorie offered, "but some men, when they get too much, go home and beat up on their wives and kids. That's no good! We used to have a guy like that in our neighborhood. She was calling the police all the time, but they never did anything. It was like she was his horse or his dog."

"There's a Humane Society to protect animals," I ventured.

"That's right!" Gloria called from the living room. She turned her black eyes on Ricki and snapped, "You'd better not beat up on me! I'll hit you with a frying pan!"

Gales of laughter filled both rooms despite the deadly serious look on her face—or perhaps because of it.

"You don't want to knock him out *yet!*" Jewel admonished Gloria. "He's brand new, practically. You just got him. You're lucky! You should take good care of him."

Ricky looked smug. "See?" he teased his wife. "You should take good care of me. I'm precious."

"We-ell," Gloria retreated, "you'd better take good care of me, too."

"Or else—the frying pan!" Dunbar laughed, pointing a finger at Ricki across the table. "How long have you two been married?"

"Long enough to be respectable," Gloria answered, patting her pregnant abdomen proudly. "Seven months pregnant—seven months married."

"Didn't waste any time, did you?" Stan remarked. "Having a family, I mean."

"Well, I could have waited a little while, but what can you do? Anyway, I think it's better to have them while you're young."

"You're lucky to be able to have 'em," Uncle Frank commented. "Some people can't have 'em."

"If you can afford 'em." Dunbar said. "If you want to give 'em a decent home and everything they need."

"Yeah," Uncle Frank agreed. "'Course, things are picking up a little now. Cars are moving a little better than they were. These government programs are putting a lot of money into the economy. This CWA program is putting lots of people to work."

While they continued to discuss some of the projects recently begun locally, such as the Thirty-fifth Street viaduct connecting the south side with the downtown area and a couple of new libraries, I brought Mr. Richmond up to date on what I had been doing since leaving high school and informing him about the people present and just where they fit into my life.

"And you're at KSEN?" he asked.

"Yes, I've been singing there since July."

"You've come a long way in just six months."

"I had to make a home for myself."

"You didn't have a home?"

"We-ell—ye-es—of sorts. I lived for a time with Aunt Belle." Since I knew she was listening while trying to appear not to by fussing over the baby, I nodded in her direction to identify her. "But they had to find other quarters— It's a long story. This isn't the time or place—"

He nodded. "I understand."

"Will you be singing today?"

"Yes." I consulted my watch. "I'll be on at 5:45. I should leave here at about five o'clock to allow for reduced bus service, today being Christmas Day."

"I'd be glad to drive you."

"O, I wouldn't want to impose on you. Don't you have other plans for the evening?"

"None. None whatever."

"Well, that would be wonderful. I'd appreciate it. I really would."

"Do you suppose they might let me in to watch? I've never seen a broadcast."

"I think I might arrange it."

"Good. Then I can bring you home, too."

"I'd like that, too."

Into the afternoon we all sat and chatted, nibbling and drinking coffee. I opened the candy and passed it around, but there was little interest.

Herman and George cleared the tables and could be heard talking as they worked in the kitchen washing dishes.

Timmy's fascination with the tree and his new toy and his excitement at viewing so many new faces had kept him from taking his customary nap. He was now becoming cross and cranky.

"I guess we'd better take him home," Marjorie said. "We still have a big dinner to go to later on."

The "good-byes" were as tedious as the greetings. There were "thanks" and kisses and hugs.

"It's a Christmas I'll never forget!" Joe exclaimed.

"You said it!" the Aldersons agreed.

"Maybe things *are* getting better."

"Sure had a good time," Stan said, putting his arm around my shoulders. "Thanks for inviting us."

"I guess I'll have to be going, too," Dunbar said. "If we're going to open up at five—"

The latter remark was intended to nudge Mother and Harve, I knew. Bret, too, was part of the Tux crew.

Harve and Mother would drive Aunt Belle and Uncle Frank back to National Avenue before going back to the club.

"Do you think you might give us a couple of numbers on New Year's Eve?" Dunbar asked me as he was leaving.

"The manager has told me a public appearance might be good—'enhance my image' is the way he put it. He says it wouldn't violate the contract. Don't you have anyone signed up?"

"No. Just the regulars. If you can make it New Year's Eve, that would be just great!"

＊　＊　＊

When the elevator doors slid shut, I came back to the apartment. Still clattering in the kitchen were Herman and George. I looked about at the enlarged dining room table and the extra table, now empty. It looked out of place in the living room.

"I feel I should do something to put things to rights, but I don't feel like it."

"Come, sit down," Mr. Richmond said. "Relax for a while before you have to go on the air."

"I believe I shall do just that. I'd like a tall glass of ice water after all that syrup. Would you like one?"

"Sounds good!"

I went to the kitchen and came back with two tall, tinkling glasses on a tray, then seated myself beside him on the sofa. The sudden quiet was a balm to my ears. But for Mr. Richmond's presence, I might have dozed.

"Did I hear you say you're going to sing on New Year's Eve?" he asked.

"Yes, Dunbar asked me to come and sing at the Tux sometime, and I was successful in getting an exception to my contract from the manager of KSEN to make this personal appearance."

"The *Tux?*"

"Yes."

"Where's that? Can't say that I've heard of it."

I put my head back against the sofa and stretched my long legs out before me. I took a deep breath. This was going to be quite a lengthy explanation.

"I think I'd better start at the beginning," I said.

I'd got halfway through the story, arriving at that portion in which I had written to KSEN requesting an audition and giving them a resume of my experience, before it was time for us to leave.

"For one so young, you've had an interesting and unusual life," he remarked as we got into our coats. "How old are you now, Lindy?"

"Almost twenty. I have a birthday coming in early February. You'll lock up before you leave, please?" I asked Herman and George still working in the kitchen.

"Don't worry about a thing."

"If you'd rather finish tomorrow, that's all right with me."

"Na-a-ah! We're almost done. It's still early. Only five o'clock. That's one of the nice things about a brunch, eh? You're done early."

"Okay, Herman, and thanks so much."

As we rode through the quiet streets in Mr. Richmond's blue Chevy, we admired the decorated trees in the windows along the way.

"You'll be presenting a Christmas program tonight, I presume."

"O, yes. It's what's expected."

"Do you have any church affiliation, Lindy?"

"No. I've sung in a lot of churches, though. For weddings. The buildings—the stained glass windows are beautiful."

He nodded as he considered my comments.

I thought of Marjorie and her mother and the rift that had been caused by their religious differences.

"My—uh—ex-fiance was quite religious."

"This is the place," I interrupted while wondering if that's what came between them. "There's a parking lot behind the building."

Entering by the parking lot door, we made our way through the building to the studio. With pride, I introduced Mr. Richmond to everyone we met.

Paul immediately invited Mr. Richmond to come into the

control room with him to watch the performance, an invitation which he eagerly accepted.

The seconds ticked by. The ON THE AIR light came to life, and Don took the mike.

Floyd rippled through an opening chord, which was now so familiar to me, and we went through the usual White Owl theme. Beginning with "O, Tannenbaum," we ended the program with Victor Herbert's "Toyland." As Don made the concluding remarks, Floyd and I again picked up the theme and the ON THE AIR light went off.

When we left the building, Mr. Richmond took my arm and said, "I feel I'm in the presence of a celebrity."

"I'm just lucky."

"Have you had any training at all?"

"Very little. Just what I was given in school, and Floyd, the accompanist, gives me a few pointers from time to time."

We were in the car, backing out of the parking space. "Have you ever considered taking some lessons?"

"No, I haven't. I've been taking one day, one week at a time, not giving much thought to next year or the year after that. It has come so fast and it's been so easy. Even the apartment. I've been in it only since October."

"I see."

We drove in silence for a few blocks.

"Getting hungry?" he asked.

"A little. I didn't think I'd ever be hungry again, but that brunch was a long time ago. It's after six o'clock."

"I wonder if anything is open."

"The Tux opened at five. Maybe some others are open, too."

"We'll drive around for a while. Maybe we'll find something."

Chapter 27

I was getting hungrier every minute as we drove through the quiet streets, and feared my empty stomach would soon be protesting audibly.

"Well, my hunch was right," Mr. Richmond observed when we arrived at the Regal Room of the Lexington Hotel. "I was pretty sure they would be open tonight. People are en route, holidays or no."

He held open the leaded-glass paneled door. Deep carpeting absorbed our steps as we entered the elegant Victorian dining room. Gleaming wood-paneled walls reflected light from simulated gas fixtures. Snowy table linens, thick and soft, were a dramatic background for polished silver and delicately patterned china.

A waiter brought ice water and menus, and told us of the traditional Christmas entrée being offered today. On a dais at one side of the room, a string quartet played chamber music. A stately Christmas tree, festooned with ropes of cranberries and popcorn and lavishly decorated with glass ornaments and unlighted candles, presided over the scene like a Victorian dowager. Looking about the room, I noted others looking at me. Self-conscious, I squirmed on my chair. The chair squeaked. Mr. Richmond's eyes met mine across the table. We laughed.

"What are you laughing about?" he asked.

"I'll tell if you will."

"Okay."

"I was thinking of a day in class when you assigned a silent reading~something by Thackeray, I think~and in the heavy silence, I squirmed in my seat and it squeaked."

"And you looked right at me."

"Yes, I did. You remember? Really?"

"I do. You turned as red as a beet."

I felt myself blush even as he spoke. "It's embarrassing to be so transparent. I wish I could control it."

"Don't try. It's a very charming attribute."

I toyed with my glass. The ice tinkled.

"Why did you squirm? Was there something in the text that made you uncomfortable?"

"Yes, as a matter of fact, there was."

"You don't have to talk about it if you don't want to."

"I'd rather not."

"Did it have anything to do with me?"

"No."

"Shucks!" he said. "I was hoping you had at least a schoolgirl crush on me."

"O, I did! We all did!"

He smiled broadly, his brows raised in surprise.

"But you were off limits to us," I continued. "You were engaged, remember? It even said so in the school paper. It was right there, black on white."

"So it was. That seems like a long time ago. It's as though I was a different person," he reminisced.

My mind flew back as I remembered how enamored of Matt I was at that time. "I feel the same."

The waiter brought our dinners, hot under silvery domes. I watched with interest while he expertly served our table, then discreetly withdrew.

The cuisine behind the scenes equaled the elegance of the dining room, and we were both soon absorbed in the enjoyment of the feast before us.

"Do you intend to continue to teach at the high school?" I asked.

"It's the kind of work I love—teaching. And it's been a good place to be during the past few years—getting paid in scrip notwithstanding. Better scrip than nothing. I think that phase is over, anyway. Whether I'll stay at the high school or not," he continued, "I'm not certain. I'm a graduate student, continuing my studies on a part-time basis."

"Where are you studying? Here in the city?"

"During the school year, yes. There are some courses I can get here. I spend the summers in Madison at the University."

"You're very busy, then."

"Yes. Too busy, I'm afraid. Not much time for a social life."

I nodded. Was it a factor in the broken engagement? I wondered.

"I suppose you have lots of dates," he surmised.

"Well, there's Bret. He plays in the band at the Tux. He's been very helpful to me. He played accompaniment for me when I auditioned at KSEN and rehearsed with me, too."

I told him of rehearsing at the speakeasy during the day when no one was around because of having no piano at home. "He's a good friend. We take in a movie occasionally—that's all. Have you dated since the engagement ended?"

"No. Just been too busy to think about it. I'm not really broken-hearted about it—the break-up, I mean. All things considered, it was for the best."

I nodded.

"Did you have any boyfriends in high school?"

"One. I dated Matt Dorsey for awhile. Do you remember him?"

"Athlete, wasn't he?"

"Yes. Valedictorian, too."

"You're right! I remember. Do you see anything of him now?"

"No. Haven't seen him for—" I thought back to the night, "more than two years, now."

"Things surely change a lot in the space of two years, don't they?" he mused. "You've really come a long way since you sat in my classroom—in a squeaky seat."

We smiled, remembering.

"Apparently you have a great gift to have done so well without training. A good teacher would help you enhance what you have. I really would like to see you get some good coaching over at the college. I hear their music department is one of the best in the state—equal to Madison."

"I have never looked into it. In fact, I don't really know how to go about it. What's the first thing I would have to do, Mr. Richmond?"

"My name is Russell," he smiled. "It depends on what you want. If you just want vocal lessons, that's one thing. If you want a degree in music, that's something else."

A degree in music?

The waiter came and removed the dishes from the table, leaving a dessert menu.

Mr. Rottman advised me to do exactly what Mr. Richmond, *Russell*, was recommending now. A million possibilities clamored for attention.

When the waiter brought my lemon meringue pie, I was deep in reflection on the hopelessness which had pervaded my thinking—all of my classmates' thinking—during those high school years. To aspire to college was unrealistic—out of the question for a person such as I.

While the coffee was poured, Russell said, "You might call the Admissions Office—tell them what you have in mind. Or I could look into it for you if you'd like me to. Of course, everybody's on Christmas vacation right now—but after the first of the year, when everything's back in full swing—"

"Yes," I said with conviction. "I'd like you to look into it for me—if you will, please?"

"I'd be happy to." He reached across the table and squeezed my hand. "I'm glad you're not quite as self-sufficient as you seem."

Russell left me at the elevator with a warm handshake that night. We exchanged thanks, he for the brunch, I for the dinner. Why was it so hard to think of him as *Russell?* After taking my phone number, he assured me that I would be hearing from him as soon as he had anything to report from the college.

As I opened the door of my apartment, I found a lamp glowing in the living room and the kitchen clean and orderly, everything in its place. Bless Herman and George! Even the table had been restored to its original size, the leaves neatly stored under the table top where they had been before.

It was early. Only nine-thirty. I turned on the Christmas tree lights and sank into an overstuffed chair to reflect on the events of the day. The colored lights, the gentle movement of the foil icicles had a hypnotic effect. Drifting in a state of reverie, eyes almost closed, I viewed through my lashes a diffused image of great beauty. *Where are you going?* The question surfaced from the depths of my subliminal mind. *Where are you going?*

✸   ✸   ✸

The week sped by. The New Year's Eve Gala at the Tux loomed ahead. I prepared a program of the best of '33: *Smoke Gets In Your Eyes, Everything I Have is Yours, Inka Dinka Doo,* and a few popular holdovers from '32, such as *Night and Day,* and *April in Paris.* Christmas had been celebrated with a degree of solemnity and restraint, but New Year's Eve was to be a Roman holiday. Its falling on Sunday, as it did this year, afforded plenty of opportunity for revelry long before "the witching hour." Consequently, when I arrived at the Tux for a ten o'clock performance, the experienced, as well as the *nouveau connoisseurs,* were already "in their cups."

Because this was my first personal appearance since becoming a local radio personality, I selected a flocked taffeta dress, full skirted, floor length, in an American Beauty Rose shade. Huge leg-o'-mutton sleeves, the vogue of the moment, broadened my shoulders and tapered my torso. A rolled collar spanned my throat, then plunged down my bare back into a V which ended at my waist.

While hanging my coat in the wardrobe room provided for the help, I felt him behind me. His hand touched my waist. He kissed my exposed back. Startled, I turned to find Dunbar in a tux, drink in hand.

"Had anything yet today?" he asked, raising the glass.

"No. Of course not."

"I brought this just for you."

"Thanks, but no. I don't think I really want any. It's bad for my voice."

"Come on. You'll sing better. It'll loosen you up a little. Help you relax."

"It'll make me cough."

"Not this stuff. It's smooth."

I smelled it and wrinkled my nose. "Well,—" I hated to be a prude about it. I took the glass from him and sipped. *Zing!* I felt a burst of heat in a portion of my anatomy I had virtually disowned, but which, emphatically, had not disowned *me*. I intended to drink no more of it.

"I'll take it with me," I said. As I turned to leave, the opening strains of my first number came from the stage.

"I'll see you later," Dunbar said, winking.

I set the drink on the windowsill. Then, coming into the spotlight, I took my place before the mike to polite applause. A few well-placed ads announcing the appearance of *Lindy* of KSEN identified me to some in the audience. I apparently had been heard by many while being seen by few.

Being in the blinding spotlight was not a new experience for me. Singing in talent shows had prepared me well for the black void before me. I sang as if there was nobody there. After a lively rendition of *Between the Devil and the Deep Blue Sea* we swung into *Mood Indigo* while dancers emerged from beneath potted palms and swayed dreamily beneath a star-studded sky.

As my eyes adjusted to the light, I began to discern figures standing along the walls. Mother was near the stage at my left and Harve stood toward the back of the hall. I was surprised to see Dunbar among the listeners since he was much in demand at the bar, not that he was needed there.

I left the stage to a much healthier round of applause than had greeted me at the beginning. As I walked past Bret at the piano, he extended one hand and touched my arm.

"And to think I knew her when~" he smiled.

Chapter 28

The air was heavy with cooking odors from the kitchen, winey barroom smells and blue with cigarette smoke. My throat was dry. I sought out the relative quiet of the wardrobe room and found the glass on the windowsill. There I sipped until it was gone.

In the kitchen I found my mother talking to the chef.

"I saw your performance," she said, and almost in the same breath, "Do I smell liquor on your breath?"

"Probably." The glass was still in my hand. "Dunbar brought me a drink as soon as I had my coat off. I've had just one."

She scowled a worried scowl. "Do you know what I'm thinking?"

"Yes, I think so."

"I'm thinking of the night you went into a tantrum because Harve was a bootlegger."

"I remember."

"Have you changed your mind? About 'booze,' as you called it then?"

"No. Not really. I just didn't want to offend Dunbar. I guess I didn't handle it very well. What should I have done?" It was the first time in several years that I had asked any advice of my mother.

"Situations become difficult at times," she admitted. "Would you like to have me speak to Dunbar? You're not twenty-one yet."

"No. I'll deal with it myself. Chances are he won't offer me any more."

"If you have a dry throat, come to the kitchen."

"Okay, Shorty!" I put my arm around her shoulders, then bent and kissed her cheek.

"Shorty!?" she laughed. "I think you've had one too many already!"

On stage, a huge clock had been a focal point of interest throughout the evening. Tension and noise mounted during the final minutes of the old year. The orchestra stopped playing while the crowd counted off the final seconds. At midnight, "Happy New Year!" was screamed, shouted, gestured and even whispered at a few tables where lovers, isolated in the caverns of their alcohol-fueled desire, shared languorous kisses with abandon, oblivious to the crowd around them. A spot illuminated a glittering 1934 above the stage, and the orchestra swung into *Auld Lang Syne.* The noise level increased to a roar.

The merrymakers, in their silly hats, now brought their horns, whistles and assorted other noisemakers into full play. The cacophony was deafening.

Mother and Harve were standing nearby. It was unearthly that we should have found each other in this wild and crowded place at this moment. Harve kissed Mother. Then they saw me and we all embraced.

"Happy New Year!"

"Happy New Year to you, too, Dear."

"Better 1934!"

I sought the mirror in the ladies' lounge to check my appearance before going back on stage. As I pushed open the door of a stall, I found that someone had vomited and left a horrible mess. The sight was revolting, the smell, nauseating. Pity the unfortunate person who would have to clean it up! I was about to notify Harve when the orchestra began playing the intro to my next set. I refreshed my lipstick and quickly got out of there.

The crowd was beginning to thin. The tension was gone. It was a dreamy time, so such tunes as *I'm Getting Sentimental Over You* and *How Deep Is the Ocean* seemed appropriate. When the applause seemed to require an encore, I responded with my old favorite, *Temptation.*

As I stepped off the platform, a fellow, obviously drunk, came toward me. His hair was tousled, his tie hung loosely about his neck, his shirt collar open.

"Hi, Beau'ful!" he slurred as he staggered my way, glass in hand. The odor of whiskey hung about him like a fog.

Without answering, I pushed past him on my way to the kitchen.

"Hey, goddam! Who'n hell do you think you are anyway?" he shouted after me.

Another patron placed a hand on his shoulder. "Hey!" he admonished quietly. "Calm down! Lay off!"

"The hell I will," the drunk argued as he clumsily pushed the other's hand away. "She's got no goddam business snubbin' *me.*"

"Just sit down here and cool off. You're drunk!"

"Drunk, am I? Why~you~" he drew his right arm back and swung a punch that hit its mark before he, along with his victim, fell across a table, knocking it over. People in the area scrambled. Men cursed and women screamed as glasses and spilled drinks flew toward them. The unfortunate patron put his hand to his nose; then, seeing blood, he reached for a handkerchief.

The witnesses looked bewildered. The dancing couples drew near to see what was going on.

Through the melee, Dunbar strode authoritatively. He was angry. "What the hell is going on here?" he demanded.

"She snubbed me, *tha's* what's goin' on," the drunk complained as those around him helped him to his feet.

"Who?"

" Your canary. She's got no goddam right to snub *me.*"

"Well, now, the lady doesn't have to speak to anybody she

doesn't want to. Just who are you anyway?"

"I'm Malcolm Prandl, *tha's* who I am. And she's gonna *pay* for this." He shook his finger under Dunbar's nose.

A voice at my side said, "Get your coat. Come on, I'll take you home."

I looked into the face of Mr. Richmond. *Russell!*

"Where did you come from?"

"Been here since about 10:30," he said, drawing me away from the crowd. "Are you through for the night?"

"Yes. I'm through."

"Do you have some way to get home?"

"I was going to call a taxi."

"You'll never get a taxi tonight. It'll take a couple of hours. My car's right outside."

As we talked, an officer in plain clothes, whom I had seen in the crowd without suspecting his real purpose, placed the drunk under arrest. The man with the bloody nose was being administered to by a woman who professed to be a nurse. Waiters and waitresses scurried to pick up the table and clean up the debris of broken glass and spilled liquor.

Since it was now well after midnight, most couples were leaving the pseudo-tropical environment for the reality of a cold Wisconsin winter night.

Russell followed as I went for my coat. When we reached the wardrobe room, Dunbar was waiting.

"What happened?" he demanded.

"He approached me, and I ignored him because he was so obviously drunk."

"Did he say anything obscene?"

"He swore a lot. His language was profane, but he was not obscene. In fact, he called me 'Beautiful.'"

"Do you know who he is?"

"No. Never saw him before in my life."

"Well~ His father sits on the board over at KSEN~as well as a lot of other boards. Just thought you'd like to know."

"O, my!" I was at first alarmed, but after thinking about it a moment, I said "I really don't know what I can do about it."

"If you can wait around for awhile," he said, looking at his watch, "I'll take you home."

"Thanks, but I've already agreed to leave now with Russell."

"Russell, eh?"

"Mr. Richmond."

Throughout this exchange, Russell stood, feet apart, hands behind his back, as I had seen him do so often before. Quietly he listened and observed. Dunbar never looked at him.

I pulled the big collar of my raccoon coat up around my face. As I put on my gloves, Dunbar said, "All right." His voice held a ring of finality. He turned and left the room.

It was cold! The car was cold. Our breath created great clouds which fogged the windows. Even inside my great coat, I shivered in my bare-back dress. My nose ran. I took off my glove to find a handkerchief in my purse and felt my fingers turn to ice.

Russell turned the key and stepped on the starter. The engine moaned and died, moaned and died again. His final attempt was met with angry whines of protest. My teeth chattered uncontrollably. The engine was silent.

"It's gotten a lot colder," Russell observed as he opened the door and got out. "I guess I'm going to have to crank." He opened the rear door and produced a lap robe.

"Here," he said, "put this around you. It'll help keep you warm. Now when it starts, give it a little gas. Not much—just a little."

"Where's the gas?"

"Right there," he said, manually placing my foot on the proper pedal, no small feat since I had to somehow get my leg around the gear-shift lever on the floor while wearing a floor-length evening gown.

"I'll try," I said. "I've never done anything like this before."

"Just a little now," he reminded me before going around to the front of the car.

I really felt sorry for him out there in the cold. I just hoped I'd do it right. I couldn't bear the thought of looking stupid to Mr. Richmond.

Exerting great effort, he turned the crank. Once. No response. Once again. A flutter. One more time. It coughed. Coughed again. I nudged the gas pedal. The engine roared to life.

Quickly he pushed the crank under the seat and got in beside me. I was relieved.

"You did it just right!" he praised me. "There's a heater. It should get warm soon."

A little fan affixed to the top of the windshield cleared it of fog. As the car warmed, the chattering subsided.

"I've been planning to buy a car in the spring, but I don't know if I can handle a crank," I commented. "What's the reason they're so hard to start when it's cold?"

"It's the oil—in part, at least. It gets stiff and thick when it's cold. They just haven't found a way yet to keep it fluid at low temperatures. That's why so many people don't use their cars during the winter."

"Gee, that's when you really need a car," I said as we left the parking lot.

Except for a few lighted Christmas trees where parties were still in progress, most of the city was now dark and quiet.

"Feeling better?" Russell asked.

"Yes. I'm much more comfortable."

"How'd you like a hamburger and a cup of coffee?"

"Sounds good."

"There's a White Tower not far from here."

"Let's take some hamburgers home. I'll make some coffee. I don't think I want to go into a hamburger joint in a formal gown."

"Good. Let's do that."

The little white tile buildings were numerous throughout the city. We had no trouble finding one.

Russell parked at the curb and left the engine running while he ran inside. Soon he returned to the car with an aromatic bagful which he handed to me. It was warm and comforting to hold and the delicious aroma stimulated our appetites.

"I can't wait to get into one of these," I said.

"They do smell good, don't they? White Tower makes a good hamburger."

"They sure do. And for a *dime!* I wonder how they do it?"

"Sign of the times. It's a good indicator of what farmers are getting for wheat and beef."

"My!" I exclaimed. I made a quick comparison. Imagine drawing a hundred-fifty a week in an economy in which you could buy a hamburger on a bun with onions or whatever you wanted for a dime!

Except for the clerk, the lobby of the Hillcrest was deserted. "Happy New Year," he said without enthusiasm as we came through. "Whatever ya got there, it sure smells good."

It was comforting to open the door and be home. We hung our coats and went into the kitchen to make coffee.

"Mind if I take off my jacket?" Russell asked.

"Why, no. Why should I mind?"

"Well, you're all dressed up—and looking beautiful, I might add."

I smiled as I busied myself filling the coffee pot and measuring the coffee. I took cups and saucers from the shelf and put the burgers on a plate. There were six of them!

"You must be really hungry," I remarked.

"I had an early dinner."

I looked up momentarily from my preoccupation with setting the table to see him without his jacket. Never before had I seen Mr. Richmond without his jacket. The fact that he was here, in my kitchen, without his jacket, seemed to be the most incredible circumstance that I had ever experienced. During all the years I was in high school, he represented to me the unreachable ultimate—like a movie star!

I recalled his readings of whole scenes of *Macbeth.* With a ring of brass in his orotund voice, he read with such expression and emotion as to bring Shakespeare to life and give his work the vigor of a blood-and-guts detective story out of a pulp magazine. Then turning to Housman's *When I was one-and-twenty*, he read with equal tenderness of youth and love, of age and remembrance.

I brought some mustard and ketchup from the refrigerator. The redolence of coffee filled the kitchen.

"I guess everything's ready," I said as I poured the coffee.

We sat silently for several minutes while we relished the juicy hamburgers and sipped the coffee, hot and strong.

"Does coffee keep you awake?" Russell asked.

"If I lie awake tonight, it won't be because of the coffee."

"Are you worried about Prandl?"

"Well—it's a darned good job. I don't want to lose it because of something I had no responsibility for."

"You won't. You're probably a more valuable property to his father than Malcolm is."

We laughed together. "I hope he sees it that way," I said.

He emptied his cup, then poured more coffee. "This is nice," he said, looking around the kitchen. "With so many people around on Christmas Day, I didn't get a very good look at the place."

"Where do you live, Mr. Rich— Russell?"

He smiled at my lapse. "I rent a sleeping-sitting room in a very nice residence over on the south side. I have a garage for my car, which is hard to find nowadays, and I take my meals out. The landlady is a widow. She keeps a nice home."

"You're comfortable there?"

"Most of the time."

"Where's your home? I mean, is this your home town?"

"No. I'm from northern Wisconsin. My father is a minister up there."

"A minister?" I pursed my lips and raised my eyebrows. "I presume you have some church affiliation here in town then."

"No, I'm afraid I've had all of that that I need for one lifetime." He drained his cup. "Too many times have I squirmed and slept on hard pews as a kid—when I would rather have been home in bed—while my folks listened to some fire-and-brimstone revivalist pound the pulpit. When my time comes, I'll have to go as I am, for better or worse. How do you feel about it?"

"I'm quite content as I am."

"It's a relief to hear you say that."

At precisely the same moment, we both yawned, despite our best efforts to conceal it from each other. We both found this amusing.

"I guess I'd better be on my way and let you get some rest," he said at last. "I'm so comfortable, I hate to think of going back out in the cold. Hope my car didn't freeze up."

I went with him to the closet to get his coat, but he helped himself and needed no assistance from me. We stood together at the door. He took my hand and drew me toward him. As if by mutual consent, our lips met. His arms held me fast. I felt his warm hands on my bare back, then inside my dress. O, Lord! What was happening here?

"O, no. Not now. Not now," I heard myself mutter as he pressed his hard body against me. Is this the same Mr. Richmond who read of innocence and ethereal love? The beauty of the rose? Was he capable of the gross and meaty passions of common men and women? Women like *me?* The discovery pleased me.

"Omigod, Russell! No! Not now. Not now."

"Sometime?"

"I—I don't know yet."

"Is there someone else?"

"No—that is—I don't know that yet either."

"I see. You need time."

"Yes."

He released me. I worried. Did I offend him?

"You must understand," I said. "I have the same need—the same desire. I want you, too, but—"

"You do? You want me?"

"Yes. Of course, but—"

"But what?"

"I'm not ready to make a commitment—not yet."

"I guess I owe you an apology," he said.

"No. No apologies. I'm flattered that you should respond to me in this way."

"Flattered?"

"Yes."

He smiled, then kissed my hand. "You're quite a woman," he said. "Quite a woman."

I sighed as I closed the door behind him.

Chapter 29

I flicked off the kitchen light and went into the bedroom. After turning on the vanity lamps, I took one last look at myself in my evening finery before disrobing for bed. The peach silk nightie caressed my elevated nipples as it slipped down over my tingling body. I was intoxicated with desire.

Lindy, I said to my reflection, *What kind of person are you? You responded to Russell tonight just as you responded to Dunbar a week ago—just as you did to Matt once upon a time.*

When I responded to Matt, Russell was an unattainable entity, and Dunbar was a myth, my reflection answered.

What about Dunbar?

I don't know. He's wedded to a kind of business—

There's a lot of money in it.

Yes, that's true. I suppose that's important.

What's more important than money?

Lots of things. Sensitivity, maturity, a sense of—citizenship—social responsibility.

Matt had all those things.

Not maturity.

How so?

He allowed others to influence his decisions.

Maturity comes with age. Matt was very young.

Matt is no longer an option. Besides, I don't think I could respond to Matt now as I did then.

Oh? Why not?

Because *I've* changed.

Are you mature?

I don't know. Only hindsight can tell me that years from now.

Might there be someone in your future—someone you haven't yet met—whom you might want even more than any of these?

Might be. Might be.

But you doubt it.

I weighed the quiet beauty of the elegant Regal Room at the Lexington against the contrived sophistication of the Tux. The vomit–splashed toilet came to mind so vividly as to make me momentarily nauseous. I saw again the bloody handkerchief of the patron who so charitably came to my defense when I was insulted by the drunk—the ugliness of the fight—the disgusting mess it created.

Yes, I doubt it, I answered my reflection.

I continued a running soliloquy while I removed my makeup. Fatigue finally overtook me as I snuggled into my welcoming bed.

※ ※ ※

It was 1934. While riding the bus to the studio on Monday, New Year's Day, I worried again about the incident involving Mr. Prandl at the Tux and wondered if there would be repercussions, but I heard no more of it as the days went by and the incident was forgotten. Then on Friday, as Floyd and I were rehearsing, Sally, the receptionist, poked her head in the door and announced that Mr. Blackstone would like to see me.

Well, here it comes, I thought. I was eager to get the confrontation behind me. I was not destitute, having put aside a considerable sum, my lifestyle notwithstanding. Surely I could get another job if worse came to worst. Purposefully, I strode into the office fortified by the knowledge that I could manage, for a while at least, with or without this job.

Miss Markowski greeted me, smiling. "They're waiting for you."

Mr. Blackstone greeted me, and smiling, gestured toward a chair. "Be seated, please."

Seated in the other chair, was Malcolm Prandl. Sober, dressed in a well-cut charcoal-grey business suit, he stood and extended his hand to me.

"Lindy, this is Mr. Prandl. I understand you two have met."

"Not really," Mr. Prandl said. "She's never really spoken to me. That was the problem." Then turning to me, he said, "Miss Albright, I've come to apologize. I was a boor—a rank philistine—and I'm sorry. I'd like to make it up to you somehow."

A *rank philistine?* I'd have to look that up. I stole a glance at Mr. Blackstone and saw that he, too, was trying to keep a straight face. Wouldn't Mother and I have a chuckle over that?

"I'm quite willing to forget the whole incident."

"O, no! I caused you pain and embarrassment. You must at least allow me to take you to dinner."

"That really isn't necessary," I said while backing toward the door as unobtrusively as possible. "I'm satisfied with the apology. It was nice of you to take the time to come here and do this. Now, I'd like to get back to rehearsal." I nodded to Mr. Blackstone and said "Excuse me, please," and backed out the door.

❋   ❋   ❋

Russell called on Saturday. "I hope I didn't interrupt anything," he began.

"No. Nothing important."

"Have you recovered from New Year's Eve?"

"O, yes. Quite. I've been working all week. Or haven't you been listening?"

"I've been listening." Pause. "How would you like to take in a movie with me this evening.?"

"I'd like that. Which one do you have in mind?"

"*One Night of Love* is playing at the Strand."

"Is that a good one?"

"The reviews are good."

"Who's in it?"

"Let's see."

I heard sounds of rattling newspapers.

"Grace Moore—she's from the Met, you know—and Tullio Carminati."

"Sounds good. I'd like to see that."

"There's a showing at nine o'clock. Suppose I pick you up at eight."

"Fine."

Happily, I went back to the small bedroom, where I had set up an ironing board, and continued my chore. The laundry's pressing service did not always meet with my satisfaction so I frequently did some touch-up work myself. I had just finished the last piece when the intercom buzzed.

"Miss Albright?"

"Yes?"

"There's a delivery here for you. Shall I send him up?"

"A delivery?"

"Yes."

"What kind of delivery? I don't remember buying anything."

"What kind of delivery she wants to know? Flowers? The man says flowers."

"*Flowers?*"

"Yeah. Flowers."

Now who would be sending me *flowers?* Russell couldn't afford them and Dunbar wasn't the type.

"All right. Send him up."

I put the ironing board away, set the iron on the drain board of the sink and waited for the doorbell.

"Miss Albright?"

"Right here." I held two dimes out to him as I took the box from him.

"Thanks!" he smiled, and caught the elevator before it went

back down.

I shut the door and, puzzled, opened the box. A dozen long-stemmed American Beauty roses! A dozen! At this time of year. Must have cost a fortune! While I enjoyed a few luxuries, I was still not too far removed from my beginnings to appreciate the value of a dollar and to have some views about what constituted frivolity.

They were gorgeous! I buried my face in their delicate petals and inhaled deeply of their fragrance. Then I saw the card. Written with a fine point pen in a precise hand, it read:

*Since you won't grant me the pleasure
of your company at dinner, I offer these
roses in apology.
Malcolm Prandl*

O, my! I thought I'd heard the last of that incident. They looked beautiful in the large glass pitcher brought down from the top shelf of the cupboard, and imparted their distinctive perfume to the entire apartment. What a shame I wasn't in love with Malcolm Prandl! I imagined the tender feelings such a gift would evoke coming from someone I really cared for. I placed them on the dining room table.

❋   ❋   ❋

I complimented myself on being ready on time as I sat comfortably reading a magazine. From a Chicago radio station, the Palmer House String Ensemble played softly.

"Come in! Come in!" I responded to the doorbell as I opened the door. "Is it cold out there tonight?"

"Not bad, really," Russell remarked. "Well, well! What have we here?" he asked, noting the roses.

"They just arrived. Aren't they beautiful?"

"Yes, quite beautiful."

Silence.

"Is it your birthday or something?"

"No. They're from Prandl."

"Who?"

"Malcolm Prandl. Remember? The fellow who created the ruckus at the Tux on New Year's Eve?"

"O-o-o."

"He came to the studio and apologized. He invited me to dinner but, of course, I said 'no'."

"You said 'no' ?"

"Yes. Here, read the card."

"Hmph! Why'd you say 'no' ?"

"I don't know. Just didn't want to, I guess. I wouldn't be comfortable with him."

"That's as good a reason as any, I suppose." After a moment's reflection, he asked, "Are you comfortable with me?"

"Mm-hmm," I nodded as I got my coat from where it lay across a chair.

"Let me help you with that," he said, taking the coat from my hands. Laying the coat aside, he held me close. His embrace was so comforting. I placed my hand at the back of his head, my cheek on his warm face. His lips found mine. I tasted his tongue. O, heavens! I was melting again.

"Do you still want to go to the movie?" he asked.

"We'd better go."

"Okay."

Nine o'clock found us comfortably seated in the darkened theater. Russell placed his hand over mine as it rested on the armrest between us. I was happy to be there with him.

As the screen came to life before us, I watched enraptured as I saw the story unfold of a young singing waitress, taken into the custody of an unrelenting coach and teacher, as she endured the rigors of his training to become one of the most idolized stars of the operatic stage. I chuckled and suffered with her as she lay on the floor visibly raising and lowering the encyclopedias placed on her diaphragm. I saw her sweat while running to achieve greater lung capacity. I heard the improvement in her delivery, over time, after endless hours of vocalizing, always seeking control—breath control, voice placement, enunciation. I experienced her discouragement as perfection eluded her.

I was struck by the fact that I was a raw amateur! I had the instrument, but no finesse in using it. Its potential was unknown. For the first time, I saw how vulnerable my position was. I could easily be replaced by any one of a dozen people in the city. The church choirs alone were a great reservoir of talent.

When the lights went up, I was slow to rise. We waited at our seats a few moments while the theater cleared, then trailed the crowd into the lobby and out into the cold night.

"I thought that was a pretty good movie, didn't you?" Russell asked after we were seated in his car.

"O! I thought it was magnificent! I'm still enthralled. I learned a lot from it."

"You learned from it?"

"O, indeed! I learned how much I don't know."

"That's always a revelation," he chuckled. "And the more you learn, the more you find you don't know."

"I think you're right, Russell. I think I should take some lessons. By the way, have you had time to get any information for me at the college?"

"Sure did. It's in my jacket pocket. I thought we might stop to have a bite to eat—if we can find anything open—and I'd give it to you then. Is that all right with you?"

"All right."

"What would you like? Something hot? Or maybe ice cream?"

"Not ice cream, please. It's too cold. Do you know of any place that makes a good bowl of chili?"

"Sure do. And it's not too far from here, either."

Some of the bulbs were burned out in the blinking sign that said EATERY outside the little restaurant. We made our way to a booth and seated ourselves on the hard wooden benches at a linoleum-covered table. The counterman brought two spotted menus and carried two glasses of water in one large hand.

Without consulting the menu, Russell asked, "Got any chili?"

"Sure have. Anything else? Coffee?" I nodded.

"Two coffees," Russell told him.

As the counterman left, Russell reached inside his jacket and withdrew a sheaf of papers. There were a number of brochures giving general information about the college and its curricula. In one of them, details were set out regarding the music department.

"I've underlined some of the pertinent information for you," Russell said, indicating the place on the page. "I'm told that this Mrs. Alford is a very good teacher. I got the phone number for you so you can call her and talk to her yourself."

The waiter brought the steaming bowls of thick chili, fragrant with spices, along with a basket of soda crackers. The coffee was good.

I gathered up the printed material and placed it in my hand-bag. "Thank you," I said between sips of hot chili. "It was awfully good of you to get this information for me. I wouldn't have known where to begin. I'll call this woman, Mrs. Alford, on Monday."

"I'll be interested in knowing what happens," he smiled.

"Tune in tomorrow," I quipped in a mock base voice, mimicking the announcers on the daytime radio dramas which I sometimes heard while I ate breakfast. "Will Lindy Albright's life take off in a new direction? Will she embark on a new course of action?"

❧ ☙

Chapter 30

The Christmas tree, which had been the sparkling centerpiece of the apartment a scant two weeks before, was now a fading relic of a bygone time. It had to come down. Never having tackled such a job before, I hardly knew where to begin, but I had put the job off as long as I dared. From the closet of the small back bedroom, I dragged the carton in which were all the partitioned boxes for ornaments and lights.

After working at it a whole morning, I still had not finished before I had to leave for rehearsal. I continued to work at it after supper finding a bird here, a rocking horse there, until the job was finished. The lead foil icicles took the most time. They were everywhere.

The next morning, I called the desk to send someone to remove the tree from the stand and dispose of it. I would phone Dunbar to pick up the decorations. I dialed his number.

"Hello!" he answered gruffly.

"Good morning! This is Lindy."

"Lindy?"

"How are you this morning?"

"All right, I guess."

His tone changed. "What can I do for you this morning, Sweetheart?"

"I've just taken down the Christmas tree."

"O, yeah?"

"Yes. And I've got all these decorations boxed and ready to go. You can pick 'em up anytime."

"Oh! Don't you want 'em?"

"Well, they're yours."

"Yeah. Well—okay. Let's see. Suppose I come for 'em tomorrow morning. Maybe we can have lunch together. I could drive you over to the studio."

I delayed answering. I should have expected this and thought it through before I called.

"Lindy? You still there?"

"Yes, I'm here. I was just trying to remember if I had something to do tomorrow, but I guess that will be all right. I'll look for you tomorrow."

"Okay, Sweetheart. See you then."

❋　　❋　　❋

I had been cutting the stems of the roses and giving them fresh water daily, but one by one, they withered and died. Today, after more than a week, there were only three left. Tight buds when delivered, they were now in full bloom and fragrant. As I tenderly cupped them in my fingers and inhaled their lovely perfume, Dunbar arrived.

"You look as good in the morning as you do in the spotlight," Dunbar commented as he appraised me in my dark blue-and-grey plaid suit.

"Well, thank you! The carton is in the living room on the floor," I said as I walked in that direction. "It's not very heavy, just bulky."

"Later." He dismissed it with a wave. Then noting the roses, he said, "Where'd the flowers come from?"

"Prandl."

"Who?"

"Prandl. Remember? The fellow who made the big fuss at the Tux on New Year's Eve."

"O-o-o! Yeah, I remember. Sent you three roses, eh?"

"No, there were a dozen. This is what's left--just these three. Aren't they lovely?"

He raised his eyebrows and shrugged. "Yeah. Pretty nice." He looked at his watch. "We've got a little time before lunch. Let's just sit down and talk a little while." He took my hand and led me to the sofa in the living room. "What have you been doing lately?"

"Working as usual." I sat on the edge of the sofa and turned to face him as I sat down beside him. He continued to hold my hand.

"Is that all you ever do? Work?"

"No. What have you been doing?"

"Working, too. What else is new?"

"O, I've seen a good movie."

"O, yeah? Which one?"

"*One Night of Love.*"

"O, boy!" he sighed. "That sounds like something I'd like. *One -Night of Love*--with you." He moved toward me.

"O, it's nothing like that!" I drew my hand away. "That's only the name of a song in the play. The play's about--something else."

"Something else? It's not about one night of love?"

"No. It's about a singer--and about her pursuit of a career."

"I see. And you're planning to follow her example. Is that it?"

"In a small way--that is, I've made a beginning."

He raised his eyebrows. "A beginning?"

"Yes. I've made an appointment with an instructor."

"How'd you hear about it? The movie, I mean?"

"A friend of mine called and told me about it."

"I see. Anybody I know?"

"Yes."

"Bret?"

I hesitated. Bret would be the logical assumption, of course, since we were both interested in music. I didn't want to lie to him, but I didn't want to tell him either.

"No, not Bret. *I say,*" I deliberately shifted the course of the conversation, "I'm getting hungry. Let's get some lunch."

He looked at his shoes for a moment. "Okay," he said. "I'm getting hungry myself."

The car, parked in the sun, started easily. It was warm and comfortable inside.

"This isn't the same car you had at the wedding, is it?" I asked.

"Nope. This is a new one—a Buick."

"My! It's a lovely car. You must be doing very well."

"We're doing better than I ever would have imagined."

"Very good!" I said. "Congratulations!"

"And your mother and Harve aren't doing bad either," he observed. "You're going to be a rich woman some day."

I? A rich woman? It took me a moment to comprehend the full implication of what he was saying. Since Mother and I had never had anything, I had never before given any thought to the fact that I was my mother's heir, and maybe Harve's, too.

We were driving south on Shoreline Drive. "Where are we going?"

"There's a nice restaurant I know about just south of the city. It's not far—about thirty miles."

"Thirty miles! I have a rehearsal to go to! I'll be late! Not thirty miles, please. Just stop anywhere along here. I'm not fussy. A hamburger will do."

"What time do you have to be there?"

"About one-thirty."

"You're exasperating. Do you know that?"

"What's exasperating? I have a job."

"You don't need a job."

"What makes you think I don't need a job? I have to pay the rent the same as everyone else."

He drove onto the shoulder of the road and stopped. I was angry. *Not again!* This was becoming a familiar tactic.

"Look!" he said, gesturing, "there's a place for you in this organization. If you would just consent to team up with me—and Lindy, I'm sincere when I tell you I want you more than anything—more than anything in the world."

His arm was across the back of the seat. He drew me toward him now and kissed me. "There's a fortune in that business. We're just beginning to realize the returns on our investment. You don't want to raise your children in poverty, do you?"

My children? What was he saying? It was my turn.

"Now, see here!" I began. "Let us understand each other. I like you, Dunbar. Mygod, I don't even know your first name."

"William," he interjected, "named for a fifteenth century Scottish poet, although I've never read any of his stuff. My mother's idea, no doubt. Must've thought she'd make a gentleman out o' me. Sorry I interrupted you. Go on."

"I want you to understand that I have some ideas of my own about my future, and becoming a part of *Tux, Inc.* isn't one of them. Not via investment or any other kind of contract. Have I made myself clear?"

He bit his lip and nodded. "Clear."

"Now, will you please turn this car around and take me to the studio? That's where my commitment is right now."

"What about lunch?"

"I don't feel like eating. I just want to get to work on time."

"There's still time for lunch," he said as he turned the car around. "We can at least get a hamburger and a cup of coffee, although I had something much nicer in mind."

"Okay," I said, satisfied that we were headed back toward the city.

Dunbar parked at a roadside restaurant where I ordered a club sandwich and coffee. I was preoccupied with my own agitated state of mind and paid no attention to what he ordered.

"Gad, woman! You're exasperating," he muttered across the table.

"You've got a lot of nerve thinking I'm ready to give up my career, my whole way of living, and rush into—" I couldn't say it. *Marriage?* I really didn't want to hurt him. "Just because you've got a lot of money~supposedly. There are other values besides money."

A few patrons sensed the antagonism between us and glanced at us askance from time to time. There was no response from him and I said nothing more.

For a long time we were silent as we rode back toward the city. While watching the highway roll out before us, I recognized that the incident had brought my real aspirations into focus. Whereas I had heretofore drifted and reacted, I now knew what direction I wanted my life to take. I was surprised—and satisfied, too—with my own audacity.

"Gee!" he said at last, "I thought I could tell our kids someday that their mother and I trimmed our first Christmas tree together."

"O, Dunbar! Let's not get sentimental about this, please. We can still be friends. My mother and her husband are going to be associated with you for a long time to come, and you'll meet a lot of other women."

"None like you." He placed his hand on my knee. I picked it up and tossed it back to him.

"You're a handsome, charming fellow, Dunbar. Rich, too. You won't have any trouble."

"Hmph!"

We were at the studio. I opened the door and let myself out of the car. Before closing it, I asked, "When are you going to pick up the carton?"

"What carton? Oh! oh! The ornaments. Tell you what. You keep 'em. And when your kids ask where they came from, tell 'em Uncle Bill."

"Aw! Y'know, Dunbar, you're kinda sweet."

ϑ∾ℛ

Chapter 31

"*Now*," Mrs. Alford said as she confidently struck a chord while standing before the solemnly majestic grand piano, "let's hear you do a few scales."

She was a large woman, probably about fifty years old. A few streaks of grey were evident in her thick black hair which was drawn into a pug at the back of her head. She had a Mediterranean complexion on which she had daubed some rouge and lipstick. Her brows were thick and dark. She wore a print dress of dark jewel tones accented by a string of pearls and several rings, one a diamond.

We worked in a large rehearsal room at the college. Our heels were noisy on the bare hardwood floors. Folding chairs were stacked against a wall and music stands stood crowded into a corner like a flock of cranes.

Dutifully, obediently, I followed all of her directions. As she coached me, she occasionally sang a passage to demonstrate. Her contralto voice was round and full. I sensed the depth, the power.

When we were finished, I waited with awe for her verdict.

"There's no doubt that you have the instrument—the voice. It's a good, strong voice. I'm sure you know that since you're already earning your living with it. It's a question of what you want to do with it. Do you want to continue in the pop field? Or are you aspiring to something more grand? Are you looking to perform only? Or do you plan to teach? Maybe someday in the future?

"Is there a husband and family in your future? You're a very attractive young woman. You may have to make some hard choices. The answers will determine what course of study you should embark on."

I wanted it all. I said so.

She smiled. "Some of those decisions can be made along the way," she conceded. "I'd like to work with you. There's room in my schedule for another student."

We made arrangements then for vocal lessons on each Saturday morning.

At first I practiced at the studio, but I soon found that it interfered with my rehearsals for the program. What's more, it gave the impression that I was using my employer's facility to advance my own interests, interests which extended beyond my affiliation with KSEN. Even though I practiced alone in a little used practice room, my vocalizing attracted attention and seemed to draw people into the area for one reason or another who had previously had no cause to enter it.

During rehearsal one day in February, I confided in Floyd, my faithful accompanist, that I was considering buying a piano for my apartment.

"Do you suppose you could help me find a good one?" I asked. "I really don't know what to look for."

"Most of us don't. It's only by shopping around and asking questions that we learn. I have a piano at home, and of course, there are several here which I play from time to time. Let's look them over."

So, by arrangement, I met him at the studio a couple of hours earlier than usual one day and we went from one studio to another which was not broadcasting at the time. As he played, he called my attention to the bell-like tones in the upper register of some of them as opposed to the tinny, flat sound of others. Certain features of construction were also pointed out to me.

Armed with his valuable expertise, I haunted the shops of one dealer after another where I picked up even more knowledge. After much back tracking and painful deliberation, I arrived at last at a final decision.

The delivery of the piano was as exciting to me as the delivery of my beautiful bed. After making concessions to space and the possibility that it might have to be moved at some time in the future, I settled on a small five-foot baby grand with a dark mahogany finish.

It was beautiful! It was exciting! I spent hours vacuuming, dusting, polishing my living room to make it worthy of such a splendid addition.

When the delivery men left the apartment, I gazed at my new possession with pride. Gingerly, I sat down on the shiny new bench and, even more tentatively, touched a key. The sound startled me. It was a sound I associated with the studio. It seemed out of place here.

O, how I wished I could play--really play--as Floyd played, with ease and assurance!

Russell rejoiced with me on seeing it for the first time one Saturday evening. He even sat down and picked out a tune-- something he remembered from his childhood--then chuckled at his own ineptness.

The lessons with Mrs. Alford proceeded during the winter months and into the spring. I settled into a daily practice routine vocalizing during the morning hours, then rehearsing the program numbers with Floyd during the early afternoon. I had said nothing of my studies at the studio, although I told Floyd of my final selection. He felt that I had made a good choice.

The fan mail was favorable and now arrived in larger quantities. The number of requests increased. I began to hear the difference in my own voice.

I continued to hear from Russell regularly; however, since he, too, was attending school as well as teaching, we counted ourselves lucky if we saw each other once a week. He would occasionally get student tickets to a concert or some other function at the school. At those times, we would bring each other up to date on what was going on in our lives.

Our encounters were sweet and sensuous, our yearnings more and more compelling. I dreaded the coming of his summer vacation from teaching since he would be living in Madison. Since teachers were paid only for the months they worked, he was required to live very meagerly in order to cover his expenses while he pursued his advanced degree.

One Saturday in early April, when I arrived at the college for my lesson, Mrs. Alford said, "I've been listening to your show. You've come along very well, but I think I've done about as much for you as I can. I would like you to contact Dr. Hendryx in Madison. I think he would be good for you. Is there some way you might arrange that?"

"For lessons?"

"Yes, for lessons. He's an excellent teacher."

"Taking lessons in Madison presents some problems," I declared.

"You might write to him first," she suggested. "The train makes a regular run~"

Take the train to Madison? I'd never been on a train. I'd never been out of the city~never had a place to go.

"~and what better investment can you make than in yourself? I would be happy to recommend you."

I thanked her for the recommendation and took Dr. Hendryx' address. I would write for an appointment.

I hadn't seen Russ for a couple of weeks and was beginning to feel neglected when he called on Saturday afternoon.

"Do you think you might have a few hours to spare for a lonesome bachelor this evening?"

"Aw-w-w! Poor fellow!" I commiserated. "I think I might be able to find the time. I'm pretty lonesome myself, you know."

"You, too? I expected a celebrity like you to be busy every night."

"I'm busy, all right. But it's a lonely busy."

"Anything in particular you'd like to do? Take in a show?"

"No-o. I'd like to talk."

"Talk?"

I visualized his arched eyebrows.

"Yeah. Just talk."

"Is seven o'clock okay?"

"Fine. D'you like popcorn?"

"Yeah."

"Okay. I'll make some popcorn."

I was happy to see him when he arrived that evening. The soapy, clean smell of him, his warmth, the feel of his great firm body against me as he hugged me. I responded joyously.

"Well!" he expressed surprise. "Did you miss me?"

"Sure did. What have you been up to?"

"Same old thing. School, school, school. If I'm not a teacher, I'm a student. I'm hooked, I guess." He made himself comfortable on the sofa and drew me down beside him. "What about you?"

"I can't even be original," I said. "I can only echo what you've just said."

"Maybe we're making progress. That's something." He loosened his tie and the top button of his shirt. "Mind if I take my jacket off?"

"Of course not," I said, taking his coat from him.

Returning from the guest closet, I asked, "Do you know anyone by the name of Hendryx in Madison?"

"Hendryx? I've heard of Warren J. Hendryx—never met him."

"My singing teacher, Mrs. Alford, suggested this morning that I study with him. She thinks she's done everything she can for me. I just wondered what you might know about him, if anything."

"Isn't his name in the literature I gave you?"

"That's all about the local college, isn't it?"

"Yes, but he might have some connection with the music department here. Let's have a look."

I rose to get the literature from the little back bedroom which was gradually becoming a kind of office-work room. As I flipped on the overhead light and opened the drawer of the dark, old dresser, I was surprised, glancing in the mirror, to see Russell standing behind me. He was watching me take the papers from the drawer.

"Here they are," I said, handing them to him.

He took them from me, sat down on the bed and began to page through them. I sat beside him and we went over the bulletins searching for Dr. Hendryx's name.

"Ah, here it is," Russell said, pointing to a thumb-nail biography. "It seems he's a graduate of the Milwaukee College--hmm--back in 1914. Not what you'd call a young fellow, but not old, either. Let's see. If he was twenty-two--twenty-three when he graduated, he'd be about-- Well! 1914 was twenty years ago, so he'd be about forty-two or forty-three years old. Served in the Army during the World War. He's accumulated a couple of advanced degrees since then. Let's see--University of Indiana--and Wisconsin and--a few other credits.

"So there you have it. Do you want to go and meet the man?" He lay back on the bed and yawned with abandon, stretching his arms above his head.

"I'm going to write to him and see if he will see me. Mrs. Alford is going to write a letter of recommendation."

"I'm planning to go to Madison about the middle of May. If you could arrange an appointment about that time, we could go together. Or don't you want to wait that long?"

"I just heard of him this morning. I think I should wait until Mrs. Alford's letter reaches him and give him some time to consider. If he'll hear me, the middle of May might be just about right."

He pulled me down beside him and taking me in his arms, kissed me roundly--and again. I felt his broad thigh across my torso. He drew me close.

"Do you take the train or drive?" I stroked his hair.

"It depends on the weather. By May, the roads should be pretty good. There's concrete all the way now." He kissed me softly, again, and yet again. Our tongues played together. "Although a train ride might be fun."

"Never been on a train," I mumbled while kissing him again. I touched his face, his neck. He was smooth and warm. He was unbuttoning my blouse.

I slipped my hand inside his shirt and touched his skin. I hungered for the warmth of his body.

"Lindy?"

"Yes."

His hand cupped my breast.

"Do you still want me?"

"Yes, but I'm afraid."

His lips were on my neck. "What are you afraid of?"

"I don't want to get pregnant now. My life is just beginning."

"Don't worry." He kissed my lips. "I won't make you pregnant."

My bra yielded one breast. "How can you say that? You mean—"

He kissed my breast. He was silent for a moment.

"Yes. I came prepared."

"O! You *knew* this would happen?"

"No." His voice was husky. "I've been prepared for a long time."

A clipped "O!" came from my tight throat.

He found the light switch. Turned it off.

This was *real!*

This was *now!*

Sensitized to his every move, I felt my heart pulsing in my ears.

He held me firm. His lips closed over my nipple. A flood of sensations surged from my loins and washed over me like a tide. Befogged, we removed my blouse and bra as we kissed and touched. I helped him take off his shirt and discovered the hard nipples buried in the hair on his chest.

For a long time we lay thus, caressing, exploring, tasting. When I felt his hands on my inner thigh, I dared to unfasten his belt and touch him.

Our lips clung as his hands stroked my thighs. When they came up into the soft moist warmth of my body, a gasp of pleasure escaped me.

Together, with much touching of tongues and hands, we helped each other remove any remaining barriers to intimacy. Buttons and snaps, hooks and eyes were adroitly dealt with while shoes thumped, keys rattled and a taffeta slip rustled to the floor.

At last! At last I could explore his shoulders, smooth and warm. How long I had wanted to touch him, hold him close. With my hands I measured the breadth and length of his back, and dared to caress his firm buttocks, while kissing, tasting. I held him endear-ingly, passionately. His lips and tongue caressed my body causing waves of pleasure to pulse through my being. There was no right, no wrong. Only this moment.

In a state of trembling rapture, I felt him enter me—and we made love tremulously, joyously, each feeling the heartbeat of the other, until the mounting tensions peaked to a grand *crescendo*, throbbed through a long *diminuendo* to a deep and satiate *finale*.

For a long time after, we lay near sleep, yet too excited to sleep. We continued to stroke each other's bodies while keeping a blanket over our shoulders.

When I thought he was asleep, I slipped into my bedroom and got my robe. I went to the bathroom, splashed water on my face and combed my hair, then sat on the sofa. I had been deeply moved by the experience. I needed to dwell on its significance.

I heard him get up and dress. In a few minutes he emerged from the bathroom and joined me, his unbuttoned shirt hanging loosely from his shoulders.

A black cloud of melancholy descended and enveloped me. Russell didn't know of my illegitimacy. Suppose he dumped me, too, just as Matt had? I began to cry.

Russell embraced me and stroked my hair.

"I'm sorry," I said.

"No need to apologize for being a woman."

"I didn't mean to cry."

"It's all right for a woman to cry. I understand it's a matter of hormones."

Hormones? All right. Let it be hormones. I wouldn't argue--not tonight.

"You aren't sorry, are you?" he asked.

"Sorry? No. I've needed you--wanted you for a long time. Longer than I care to admit--even to myself."

"There aren't many women these days who would admit to having such inclinations."

"Well--women have them--and they have to cope the same as men."

"You're very candid. I appreciate that quality in you."

We sat quietly, holding hands.

"Did you really have a school-girl crush on me?" he asked imp-ishly.

I chuckled. "Sure did. Never, *never* expected anything like this.

Chapter 32

Even though Mrs. Alford had not yet had a response from Dr. Hendryx when I came for my next lesson a week later, she was confident that her recommendation would be followed by an invitation to audition.

"I've selected a few of Sigmund Romberg's songs for you to work on. They're lilting and exuberant, and I think they suit your style," she stated as she showed me the music.

I had never heard the music before, but I soon became familiar with *When Hearts Are Young* and *Romance*. My favorite was *You Will Remember Vienna*, and I was soon singing them around home for my own pleasure.

On the thirtieth day of April, at a time folks thought they could take their cars out of mothballs and get out on the highways again, winter got in one of its last wallops and socked southeast Wisconsin with an ice storm. It knocked out power lines, deadened traffic signals and snarled traffic. Budding trees and daffodils were beaten by the storm. Bus service was so far off schedule that what was normally a ten-minute ride from the studio took almost an hour.

I had left the Hillcrest that day in a chilling rain. Now I stopped in the vestibule to stomp the ice from my boots. Chunks of the wet stuff stuck to my hair where it was unprotected by my hat. I brushed it from my sleeves and collar before entering the lobby and was not surprised when a chunk of ice slithered down my back.

Chilled and miserable, I almost walked past the desk when the clerk called me.

"Miss Albright! Miss Albright!"

I turned back.

"Mail for you."

"Mail? In this weather?"

"Yup!" the young man answered. "You know what they say about the mail. It goes—come hell or high water."

"I guess we've had a little of both," I remarked as I took the mail from him. "Are the elevators running?"

"Yup! Standby power plant."

"Thank goodness!"

"'Evenin', Miss," the elevator operator greeted me as I entered. "I see you made it all right."

"Yes. It's nasty out there."

"It won't last long this time o' year," he commented as he opened the doors on the top floor.

After taking off my boots, I hung my coat from the shower rod to drip into the tub. I considered going down to Herman's coffee shop for supper but opted instead for a can of soup with crackers and a cup of hot coffee. An apple for dessert would top it off.

As I sat at my kitchen table in my snugly bedroom slippers, a bowl of steaming minestrone before me, I turned my attention to the envelope the clerk had given me. The logo was from the University of Wisconsin. Beneath it was typed Dr. Warren J. Hendryx.

Dear Miss Albright:
  This acknowledges your request for an audition with a view toward becoming my student.
  Mrs. Alford, your present teacher, has also contacted me with regard to your further studies. She advised me of your present connection with KSEN of Milwaukee and suggested I listen to your show which I have done.
  I feel that an audition and interview are in order and would welcome the opportunity to meet with you and discuss the possibilities.

I can offer you a choice of two open dates: Thursday, May
17, at 3:00 p.m. or Thursday, May 24, at 2:30 p.m..
Please advise at your earliest convenience which date
is most satisfactory to you.
I look forward to making your acquaintance.
Very truly yours,

Warren J. Hendryx

Warren J. Hendryx

After supper, I went into the den and, for the first time ever, called Russell.

"Good evening," his landlady answered. I was impressed. I always just said *hello*.

"May I speak to Mr. Richmond, please?"

"Who shall I say is calling, please?"

"Lindy."

"Lindy? Lindy who?"

"Just Lindy. I think he'll know who I am."

Silence for a moment.

"Please wait a moment."

I studied *The Hunt* which hung above the desk.

"Hello!" Russell answered.

I responded to his resonant voice just as I had in high school.

"I hope I didn't disturb you."

"A welcome disturbance."

"You don't mind my calling you?"

"Mind? I thought you'd *never* call. Has something happened?"

"Well, sort of. I've had a letter from Hendryx."

"Is that so? What does he say?"

"He's given me two dates for an audition and he would like to be advised as soon as possible about which one I will use."

"I see. What are the dates?"

"Thursday, May 17, or Thursday, May 24. If those dates conflict with your schedule, I'll just take the train and get a taxi from the station to his address."

"I haven't taken a day off all year. I'd like to take the train with you. I'll simply arrange to be absent. What day is best for you?"

"I will have to make arrangements, too. I'll talk to the program director and let you know."

"Okay. See you Saturday?"

"Saturday's fine."

Floyd agreed to fill the slot with piano music on the twenty-fourth so I was allowed the day off.

I examined my wardrobe and found I owned nothing suitable for such an occasion. I was sharply reminded that less than a year ago, I was still living on National Avenue with virtually no income. Mornings of the following week were spent searching for just the right costume. I settled on a coarse linen of a color known this year as *prune*. A blouse of turquoise silk and dark brown pumps along with a matching purse and gloves completed the ensemble.

As I dressed on the morning of the twenty-fourth, I realized I had given no thought to jewelry. I fumbled through what I had, which was very little since I was not given to wearing much adornment. Still, the plain neckline was too severe.

I ran across the black onyx signet ring on the gold chain my mother had given me last year. I had never worn it. I tried it on. It was the perfect accent!

At promptly six o'clock on the morning of the twenty-fourth day of May, Russell rapped quietly at my door. The building was still asleep.

"New suit?" Russell asked, looking me over.

"Yes. I wanted to make the right impression."

"You'll do that all right. I suppose I'd better not get near you lest I disturb a hair or make a wrinkle."

"I'm not that fragile," I assured him, kissing him.

Quietly, we stepped out into the sweet freshness of the morning. I was thrilled and excited to be going on a trip—something I had never done before.

The depot, with its high, domed ceilings, its polished wood pillars and banisters, its mosaic tiled floors filled me with awe. I was fascinated by the ebb and flow of people coming in and leaving, the greetings, the departures, some happy, some tearful, the smell of leather suitcases, the nasal chant of the announcer as he called out the destinations of departing trains. I sat on one of the long benches divided by ornate iron armrests and admired the sophistication of my handsome escort as he strode toward the ticket window.

The hissing of the steam engine as we stepped onto the platform excited me. I'd never been this close to the iron mammoth before. It exuded strength and pride, not only in itself, but in the skills, ingenuity and resolve of the nation. This was my country, my world, *my time*, and I was the proud heiress of all the achievements of the past.

Stepping aboard, I felt like a child at an amusement park. I was going for a ride! The green velour-upholstered seats, the quaint light fixtures, the water bottle in its niche at the end of the car where little conical paper cups were offered from a tube, all enchanted me.

Russ sat beside me, possessively holding my hand as though, like a small child, I might get lost.

"This is fun!" I exclaimed, stimulated by this new experience.

Smoothly, imperceptibly, the train began to move. We were quickly out of the city, the late May landscape opening, then closing in about the windows as we alternately skimmed across the countryside or through a copse of trees.

The conductor, like a sailor on sea legs, strode confidently through the swaying car punching tickets at every seat. Then we relaxed to enjoy the ride.

Finding a taxi was no problem since several waited for passengers at the Madison depot. It was agreed that Russell would drop me off and then attend to some matters of his own in connection with the courses he intended to pursue during the coming summer. He would come back for me in a couple of hours. We gave the driver the address on the letterhead.

I left the cab and walked purposefully along the long walk, which wound through the parklike surroundings, toward the red brick building. I turned and waved to Russell as the cab left the curb, and realized how dependent on him I had become. I wanted him here with me, now.

My hand was on the doorknob of Dr. Hendryx's room when it swung open and a young girl dashed out, pushing me aside. We were each startled at the sight of the other.

"O! I'm sorry!" she gushed. "Did I bump you?"

"No," I laughed. "I'm okay. I jumped out of the way in time."

She was about my size and build and appeared to be about sixteen years old.

"You're sure you're okay? May I help you?"

"I'm looking for Dr. Hendryx. This is his room, isn't it?"

"O, yes," she said. "Go right in." Then turning back, she called, "Dad! Someone's here to see you. He's on the phone," she explained. "He'll be with you in a minute. Just go right in."

She smiled, then left as I stepped inside. Again, we were in a rehearsal hall, this one smaller than the one I had become accustomed to. A large desk occupied one corner of the room.

While concluding his telephone conversation, he looked up and smiled at me and waved me forward, beckoning me to a chair. I sat down and waited while he hung the receiver and rubbed his palms together, smiling.

"Well, now," he said as he rose to shake my hand, "you're Miss Albright?"

"That's right."

"I'm Dr. Hendryx. I am happy to meet you. Mrs. Alford has written me about your progress and I have heard you from KSEN a number of times."

He was a tall man, over six feet I thought, with medium brown hair and clear blue-grey eyes. A bald spot was just beginning to be visible on his pate.

"You've brought some music, I see."

"Yes, a few numbers I've been working on."

"May I see them, please?"

I took them from the leather case and handed them to him.

"Ah, yes!" he smiled. "Sigmund Romberg. Delightful stuff! Have you done any acting, Miss Albright?"

"No."

"Never participated in an operetta?"

"No. Never. Never had the opportunity."

"It's great fun. Hard work, but great fun nevertheless. Let's step over to the piano."

We went through the usual warm-up during which he put me at ease and helped me to relax. Then he sat down and played the introduction to *Romance* as though he had done it a thousand times before.

As I sang, he occasionally directed me with one hand. I somehow understood every nuance of his hands, his fingers, the expression of his face, the tilt of his head.

He made no comment but looked pleased. I thought I had done better than ever before.

Then we went into *When Hearts Are Young* and communicated as well as in the one before.

"Very good!" he commented when we finished. "Come over to the desk and tell me something about yourself."

I followed him as he walked across the room and sat opposite him as he took his chair behind the desk.

In response to his questions, I told him of the solo work I had done in high school, of the talent shows I had participated in at the movie theaters around town and how it lead to my being hired to sing at weddings and wedding dances.

As we talked, my fingers wandered to the necklace I was so unaccustomed to wearing, and I unconsciously pulled the ring back and forth on its chain as we talked and laughed.

He smiled and nodded as he listened. We talked about the wedding customs of some of the ethnic groups I spoke of and laughed easily together about some rituals that seemed strange to us. The talk drifted to ethnic art forms and he asked, "Is that necklace representative of any particular culture?"

"No," I answered, feeling my face grow hot.

"Is it an heirloom piece?"

"You might say that. It was my mother's."

"Is your mother dead?"

"No." This line of questioning caught me unprepared. "She gave it to me last year~when she got married."

A long moment of silence followed. Embarrassed, I felt obliged to fill the void. "She got it from an old boyfriend." I laughed nervously.

"It's a signet ring, isn't it?"

"Yes."

"I once had a similar one. Well," he said, rising from his chair, "let's go through *Vienna* before you leave. Since you've prepared it, I'd like to hear it."

We again took our places at the piano and, since I was now completely at ease with him, I let the lilting music pour forth with joy and abandon, bringing the song to its climactic conclusion.

Russell stood applauding at the door. Dr. Hendryx joined in the applause as he rose from the piano.

"Dr. Hendryx, I'd like you to meet my friend, Mr. Richmond," I said as we met in the middle of the room.

They shook hands acknowledging the introduction.

"There are a few more things to discuss before you leave," Dr. Hendryx said, addressing me. "About the lessons. Do you want to make that commitment now?"

"Yes, I believe so."

"Did Mrs. Alford speak to you at all about the fee?"

"No, she wasn't sure, but she gave me an approximate figure which was agreeable to me."

"Well, I think we'd better be definite about the details~the hour and the cost. Let's step over to the desk again for a moment."

Russell and I sat opposite him as he took his place. He referred to his schedule and we agreed to a Saturday morning lesson time. The fee was high, especially when the train fare was taken into account.

At last he stood and took my hand. "It's been a very pleasurable afternoon," he remarked. His eyes were on the necklace. "That ring intrigues me. Would you mind taking it off? I would like to take a good look at it."

I unfastened it easily and handed it to him.

He took it to a window and examined its face. Then he looked inside for an engraving. He tried it on. A slight effort pushed it past the knuckle. It fit!

I sat spellbound as I watched him. I felt I was on the edge of a precipice. Russell knew nothing of the ring or its history.

Dr. Hendryx gave the ring back to me while scrutinizing my face. "Is your mother's name Elizabeth?"

"Yes."

"My God! What's your birth date?"

"February 6, 1914."

His right hand covered his mouth as he sat behind his desk, his brows were drawn together in an attitude of concentration. "May, 1913," he muttered, mostly to himself. He leaned forward. "~near the end of the school year. Elizabeth was about to graduate. In June, I accompanied my mother to Germany where she visited her family for the last time. We spent the entire summer there, returning near the end of August. A good thing, too, because the following year marked the beginning of the World War in Europe. I never saw Elizabeth again."

I became oblivious of Russell. I stared at this man remembering the photo. Yes, yes, the resemblance was unmistakable. "Are you my father?" I blurted. I could wait no longer.

"Is that what your mother told you?"

"She told me this ring belonged to my father." I was upset~near tears.

"It's my ring."

Great sobs shook my shoulders as I wept uncontrollably. Russell, though completely bewildered, placed his arm around my shoulders in an attempt to comfort me.

The girl I had seen earlier appeared in the doorway. "Dad, will you be leaving soon? I'd like a ride home."

"Come in," he said, gesturing.

I'd been looking in a mirror enough years to see the stunning resemblance between us. We were all astonished.

She came forward. The questioning expression on her face turned to alarm when she saw that I'd been crying.

"Well, what's the matter with everybody?" she asked. "You look as though you've seen a ghost."

"We have," her father said. "Can you find something to do for a little while. I still have a few things to discuss with Miss Albright."

"All right!" she snapped. "I'll be out in the hall."

જીજી

Chapter 33

The ball was clearly in Dr. Hendryx's court. He sat behind his desk, his hands folded in his lap, and studied his thumbs.

I had a billiard ball in my throat. It hurt.

Poor Russell! What had I dragged him into? He must have been at least uncomfortable. His expression revealed nothing. His arm rested on the back of my chair. In a protective attitude, he leaned toward me.

"Do you want me to leave?" he whispered hoarsely.

"No! No! Please stay." I took his hand.

Somewhere in the room, a clock ticked relentlessly.

At last Dr. Hendryx stirred in his chair. "I don't know what to say. I'm as shocked by this development as I know you must be. You've got to believe me when I say I never knew.

"It occurs to me that, since we can't go back, we can only go forward from this moment. There are many questions to be answered. Perhaps when we have more answers, we will know better how to proceed.

"In the interim, Miss Albright~Lindy~there will be no charge for the lessons. That goes without saying. Further, I will provide you with a book of railroad tickets to cover your transportation costs. You may look for them in the mail.

"I'm going to have to ask both of you to tell no one of this situation until—well—I would like more information in the first place—information that you're not able to supply. What's more, I should prefer to be frank with my wife and daughter about this matter, but it's going to take some time. I can only hope you understand."

"I would like to tell my mother, if you have no objection."

"She didn't know of your coming to see me today?"

"No. She's very busy in her own life. I don't see a great deal of her anymore. In fact, I haven't lived with her since I was about seventeen."

"And you're twenty now." He shook his head. "My! I have so many questions! Judging by what I see, I'd say she reared a fine daughter."

He leaned back in his swivel chair behind the desk and looked past us through the windows at the back of the room.

"How long did you know my mother?" I asked.

"We met at a 'get-acquainted' tea given on campus by one of the sororities," he began. "All the young men went to meet the young ladies. They served hors d'oeuvres and punch and tea and little tea cakes. We dressed to the hilt for the occasion. Elizabeth wore a blue gown with a lace collar. I remember a wide blue sash tied in a big bow at the back. Her hair was dark and shiny."

"What happened then?"

"We spent the evening talking together. She was aspiring to a Teacher's Certificate. I was in liberal arts at the time, majoring in music. At the end of the evening, I walked her back to her aunt's home a few blocks, maybe a mile away, where I kissed her good-night."

"Did you see her after that?"

"Yes. We ran into each other frequently on campus, of course, and soon were making arrangements to meet here and there.

"She was poor. The oldest child of a large family, she told me her parents, brothers and sisters were sacrificing a great deal just to keep her in clothes and books. She lived gratis with her father's sister and her husband. Since they were childless, they were paying her tuition in the hope that once Elizabeth was employed, she would be able to make some financial contribution to the large family back home in rural Wisconsin."

"Did you ever meet her aunt and uncle?" Russ asked.

"No. They were very strict with Elizabeth—kept her on a very 'tight rein,' so to speak. Never having had any children of their own, they had little tolerance for her youthful exuberance. Her natural spontaneity was squelched at every turn. She was required to walk sedately, to speak in modulated tones, to control her laughter, to hold her fork in a certain way, to eat her soup thus and so. They were sure that since she came from the country, she must be a peasant and they were determined to make a lady of her."

"Poor Mother!" I whispered in spite of myself.

Russ shifted his position.

"Indeed! Poor Mother!" Dr. Hendryx echoed. "She told me that our times together were the only times she could be herself—express herself naturally—without fear of being corrected or reprimanded for some infraction or another. We laughed and played like children when we were together." He chuckled as he remembered.

"Of course, all our meetings were clandestine, and since Elizabeth was fundamentally honest, she found the constant need to resort to subterfuge deplorable.

"What's more, she missed her family terribly. Being accustomed to the squabbles, the competition, the play, the general rough-and-tumble of a house full of children," he gestured as he gazed out the window, "she found the atmosphere in her aunt's home stultifying.

"In May, we had a spell of unseasonably warm weather. It lifted the spirits of everyone. Elizabeth met me in Lake Park one evening on pretext of attending a farewell party for a sorority sister. She was worried about the up-coming exams. She feared her unhappiness had affected her ability to concentrate and spoke in the most dismal terms of the consequences should she fail.

"We lingered in the park until darkness overtook us. I attempted to console her and~well~one thing led to another."

Dr. Hendryx paused to scratch his ear.

"There was a pavilion in the park not yet open for the summer. We found an unlocked door and made our way inside. There in the blackness of the spring night, we made love."

He brought his clasped hands to his forehead.

I felt his torment. I was reminded of Matt and myself.

Recovering his composure, Mr. Hendryx went on. "I gave her my ring that night. It was meant to be a token of my eternal regard for her~nothing more. I couldn't be serious about her. She was the first in her family to complete high school. My family would never have accepted her. She would have been miserable."

The parallel was astounding! In pain, I inhaled audibly.

Russ stirred in his chair. "We're going to have to leave soon if we're going to catch that train."

Dr. Hendryx stood and drew a set of keys from his pocket. "My car is right behind the building," he said. Dr. Hendryx touched my back in a gesture of comfort as we walked to the door.

"I will look forward to seeing you next Saturday," he said. "I will expect to see you regularly from now on."

We stepped out into the late afternoon of a May day. The leaves at the tops of the giant old trees on the lawn whispered their ceaseless gossip as we walked toward Mr.Hendryx' car.

There she is! There she is! they seemed to say.

She's the child! She's the child!

❋   ❋   ❋

The clacking rails, the sway of the car, the passing scene brought on a state of reverie. We lapsed into a dreamy silence. I began to think ahead to my next meeting with my father. *My father.* The words had a strange ring to me. I was surprised to find that Russ was apparently thinking along the same line.

"It's hard for me to believe that in all the years you were growing up, you didn't ask your mother his name," Russ broke the silence.

"I did, when I was very small, about four or five."

"She wouldn't tell you?"

"She said it was a secret."

"Hm-m. I wonder why. Don't you?"

"I did. But just before her marriage last June, at the time she gave me the ring, she gave me some insights as to why she didn't want his identity known. So I understand now."

"Do you want to tell me?"

"Well, she recognized the differences in their social backgrounds and sensed they just didn't mesh. She felt she would have been looked down upon by his family and that all of us would be unhappy."

I gazed unseeing through the window and relived a scene from long ago.

"Mommy, all the kids have daddies. Why don't I? Where is my daddy?"

"He's gone."

"Where did he go?"

"He went away."

"Where did he go when he went away?"

"I don't know."

"Why did he go away? Didn't he like us?"

"He didn't know you. He would have liked you if he'd known you."

"Why didn't he know me?"

"Because you hadn't been born yet."

"Mommy?"

"Yes?"

"What was his name?"

"To you, his name would be Daddy."

"What would his name be to you?"

"It's a secret."

"Why is it a secret?"

"It's important that no one know."

"Do you know?"

"Yes, I know."

"Why won't you tell me?"

"For the reason I just gave you. No one must know."

We had ridden quietly for a long time before I broke the silence.

"Well," I sighed, "now you know."

"Yes, and now you know, too."

"I've always known."

"I don't understand. You always knew he was your father?"

"No. I didn't know that until today."

"What, then, have you always known?"

"That I'm illegitimate--an illegitimate child."

"Why does that disturb you?"

"It makes a difference to a lot of people."

"Has that been your experience?"

"O, yes!" I declared emphatically.

"In what way? Give me a f'rinstance."

I thought of Matt and his family. I really didn't want to go into that with Russ.

"Well," I hedged, "it's important to a lot of people."

"I wonder if it's as important to 'a lot of people' as it is to you."

"You mean I'm imagining it?"

"You could be. You could be giving it greater importance than it deserves."

We were silent a few more minutes. Then he said, "D'you know what my father says about illegitimate children?"

"No. What does he say?"

"He says there aren't any. He says there are only illegitimate parents."

I smiled. It was a beautiful thought, one that relieved me of all stigma and placed it on my mother--and now Dr. Hendryx. I chuckled out loud. Yet I couldn't judge them too harshly. I was no better than they, only more fortunate.

"How do you feel about this child of two illegitimate parents?"

"How do I feel?" He turned my face toward him and looked squarely into my eyes. "Need you ask?"

"You mean it doesn't matter to you?"

"Not a whit."

"O, Russell," I began to cry again. "I've been so worried!"

"Worried?"

"Yes. About how you'd react when you found out. I was so afraid~"

"Afraid?"

"I was sure you'd dump me."

"I mean that much to you?"

"Well~yes~of course! What did you think?"

"I hoped I did~but~"

"But what? Do you think I go to bed with everybody?"

"Well, you've got admirers sending you roses~fellows who wear diamonds and drive big, new cars~and offering lots of things that I can't offer you~yet. Maybe never. You don't become a teacher to get rich, you know.

"Take Dunbar, for instance. He has lots of money. He'll probably propose to you one of these days."

"He already has."

"A woman would be a fool not to marry a man with his money~and good looks, too. Think of what it would mean~ He has?"

"Yes. He has."

Russell blanched.

"What did you say?" he asked, his brows drawn together.

"I said 'no.'"

He took my hand in both of his and kissed me gently. The conductor smiled as he picked up the pink ticket above our seat.

"There's just one thing I need to know," Russ said.

"Yes? What's that?"

"How do you feel about a civil ceremony?"

"Are we both talking about the same thing? What kind of ceremony?"

"Wedding ceremony, of course."

"A civil *wedding* ceremony?
He looked dubious. "Yeah."
"They're traditional in our family."
"Traditional?!"
"Go back at least one generation."

৵   *The End*   ৎ

SOURCES

The author acknowledges with gratitude the following
sources of information:

The Oxford History of the American People
by Samuel Eliot Morrison
New York - Oxford University Press (1965)

The Encyclopedia of American Facts and Dates
Eighth Edition - by Gorton Carruth
Harper & Row (1987)

American Chronicle - Six Decades of American Life
by Lois Gordon and Alan Gordon
Atheneum - New York (1987

FDR - A Centenary Remembrance
by Joseph Alsop
The Viking Press - New York (1982)

The Depression Years
As Reported By The New York Times
Edited by Arleen Keylin
ARNO Press - New York (1976)

Firestone Road Atlas and Vacation Guide
by Rand McNally Company
Chicago/New York (1983)□

Front Page - 1839 - 1988
Wisconsin State Journal, Madison, Wisconsin
Edited by William C. Robbins
James E. Burgess, publisher   Frank Denton, editor (1988)

Microfilms of The Milwaukee Journal (1931 - 1934)
Courtesy of Milwaukee Public Library
Milwaukee, Wisconsin

continued

Encyclopedia Brittanica
The University of Chicago
William Benton, Publisher (1972)

The Random House Dictionary of the English Language
Second Edition Unabridged (1987)

Literature and Life - Book Four
Greenlaw--Miles
Scott Foresman and Company (1929)

College Business Law
Rosenberg-Ott
Gregg Publishing Division
McGraw-Hill Book Company (1961)

It Might As Well Be Spring
Margaret Whiting
Morrow Publishing   (1987)
New York, NY

About the Author

Lucille Goldschmidt Larson is a native of Milwaukee, Wisconsin, where the story of *NATIONAL AVENUE* unfolds. A 1984 graduate of *The Institute of Children's Literature*, Redding Ridge, Connecticut, Ms. Larson has also studied creative writing at Milwaukee Area Technical College and has participated in workshops at Alverno College, Milwaukee. Her work has been published in Alive!, (fiction,) House of White Birches, The Milwaukee Sentinel, The Milwaukee Journal, Cappers, Fireside Companion, The Advocate (fiction, Prattsville, NY), Milwaukee Journal-Sentinel, Good Old Days and other regional papers. Her entry in the 1992 *Yarns of Yesteryear* Contest, sponsored annually by the University of Wisconsin-Madison, ranked among the top ten.

After rearing two sons and three daughters, to whom this book is dedicated, Ms. Larson attended Spencerian College in Milwaukee. For fourteen years, she worked as a law stenographer in the District Attorney's Office of Milwaukee County.